ECDL

Advanced Spreadsheets for Microsoft® Office XP & 2003

We work with leading authors to develop the strongest educational materials in computing, bringing cutting-edge thinking and best learning practice to a global market.

Under a range of well-known imprints, including Prentice Hall, we craft high quality print and electronic publications which help readers to understand and apply their content, whether studying or at work.

To find out more about the complete range of our publishing, please visit us on the World Wide Web at: www.pearsoned.co.uk

ECDL

Advanced Spreadsheets for Microsoft® Office XP & 2003

Sharon Murphy
and Paul Holden

PEARSON
Prentice Hall

Harlow, England • London • New York • Boston • San Francisco • Toronto • Sydney • Singapore • Hong Kong
Tokyo • Seoul • Taipei • New Delhi • Cape Town • Madrid • Mexico City • Amsterdam • Munich • Paris • Milan

Pearson Education Limited
Edinburgh Gate
Harlow
Essex CM20 2JE
England

and Associated Companies throughout the world

Visit us on the World Wide Web at:
www.pearsoned.co.uk

First published in Great Britain 2006

© Rédacteurs Ltd 2006

All rights reserved. No part of this publication may be reproduced, stored in a retrieval system, or transmitted in any form or by any means, electronic, mechanical, photocopying, recording or otherwise, without either the prior written permission of the publisher or a licence permitting restricted copying in the United Kingdom issued by the Copyright Licensing Agency Ltd, 90 Tottenham Court Road, London W1T 4LP.

All trademarks used herein are the property of their respective owners. The use of any trademark in this text does not vest in the author or publisher any trademark ownership rights in such trademarks, nor does the use of such trademarks imply any affiliation with or endorsement of this book by such owners.

The screenshots in this book are reprinted with permission of Microsoft Corporation.

European Computer Driving Licence, ECDL, International Computer Driving Licence, ICDL, e-Citizen and related logos are trade marks of The European Computer Driving Licence Foundation Limited ("ECDL-F") in Ireland and other countries.

Pearson Education Ltd is an entity independent of ECDL-F and is not associated with ECDL-F in any manner. This courseware publication may be used to assist candidates to prepare for ECDL tests. Neither ECDL-F nor Pearson Education warrants that the use of this courseware publication will ensure passing of ECDL tests. This courseware publication has been independently reviewed and approved by ECDL-F as complying with the following standard:

Technical compliance with the learning objectives of ECDL Advanced Syllabus Version 1.0.

Confirmation of this approval can be obtained by reviewing the Courseware Section of the website www.ecdl.com.

The material contained in this courseware publication has not been reviewed for technical accuracy and does not guarantee that candidates will pass ECDL tests. Any and all assessment items and/or performance-based exercises contained in this courseware publication relate solely to this publication and do not constitute or imply certification by ECDL-F in respect of ECDL tests or any other ECDL-F test. Irrespective of how the material contained in this courseware is deployed, for example in a learning management system (LMS) or a customized interface, nothing should suggest to the candidate that this material constitutes certification or can lead to certification through any other process than official ECDL/ICDL certification testing.

For details on sitting ECDL tests and other ECDL-F tests in your country, please contact your country's National ECDL/ICDL designated Licensee or visit ECDL-F's web site at www.ecdl.com.

Candidates using this courseware publication must be registered with the National Licensee, before undertaking ECDL tests. Without a valid registration, ECDL tests cannot be undertaken and no ECDL certificate, nor any other form of recognition, can be given to a candidate. Registration should be undertaken with your country's National ECDL/ICDL designated Licensee at any Approved ECDL Test Centre.

ECDL Advanced Syllabus Version 1.0 is the official syllabus of the ECDL certification programme at the date of approval of this courseware publication.

ECDL Advanced Spreadsheets for Microsoft® Office XP & 2003 may be used in assisting students to prepare for a European Computer Driving Licence (Advanced) Examination. None of the European Computer Driving Licence Foundation Limited, Rédacteurs Limited or the publisher warrants that the use of *ECDL Advanced Spreadsheets for Microsoft® Office XP & 2003* will ensure passing the relevant examinations.

Rédacteurs Ltd is at www.redact.ie

ISBN-10 0-131-86654-0
ISBN-13 978-0-13-186654-6

British Library Cataloguing-in-Publication Data
A catalogue record for this book is available from the British Library

Library of Congress Cataloging-in-Publication Data
A catalogue record for this book is available from the Library of Congress

10 9 8 7 6 5 4 3 2 1
10 09 08 07 06

Typeset by 35
Printed and bound in Great Britain by Henry Ling Ltd, Dorchester

The publisher's policy is to use paper manufactured from sustainable forests.

Preface

What is ECDL?

ECDL, or the European Computer Driving Licence, is an internationally recognized qualification in information technology skills. It is accepted by many businesses as a verification of competence and proficiency in computer skills.

The ECDL syllabus is neither operating system nor software specific.

For more information about ECDL, and to see the syllabus for *ECDL Module 4, Spreadsheets, Advanced Level*, visit the official ECDL website at www.ecdl.com.

About this book

This book covers the ECDL Advanced Spreadsheets Syllabus Version 1.0, using Excel XP or Excel 2003 to complete all the required tasks. Most of the procedures are identical in both applications, where they differ, the text indicates the alternative procedures for each version. Most of the screenshots are taken from Excel XP – there may be minor graphical variations in Excel 2003.

It is assumed that you have already completed the spreadsheets module of ECDL 3 or ECDL 4 using Excel, or have an equivalent working knowledge of the product.

The chapters in this book are intended to be read sequentially: each chapter assumes that you have read and understood the information in the preceding chapters and each exercise builds on the results of previous exercises. The exercises should be completed in order.

Additional exercises, labelled *Over to you*, have been posed for you to complete. These exercises provide limited guidance as to how to go about performing the tasks, since you should have learned what you need in the preceding exercises. Some of these exercises are marked as mandatory and others as optional. The changes you make in the mandatory exercises are used in later exercises in the book.

> **Note:** Although it is recommended that you work through the book to generate your own result files, to facilitate 'dipping-in' and quick revision, worked exercises are provided on the accompanying CD. Each exercise in the book indicates at the start which worked exercise can be used as a starting point instead of your own file, if you prefer to use these.

Hardware and software requirements

To complete all of the exercises in this book, you should install Excel XP/2003, Microsoft Query and Word XP/2003.

Please check the Microsoft website (www.microsoft.com) for details of the hardware requirements for your chosen operating system and Office version – the specific requirements depend on your selected combination.

You will need *up to* 6MB of free space on your hard disk for the exercise resources and your worked solutions, depending on whether or not you choose to save a separate file after each exercise or copy the solutions from the CD to your hard disk.

Typographic conventions

The following typographic conventions are used in this book:

Bold face text is used to denote command names, button names, menu names, the names of tabs in dialog boxes and keyboard keys.

Italicized text is used to denote cross-references within the book, as well as field names, options in drop-down lists and list boxes, dialog box names, areas in dialog boxes, toolbars, cells in spreadsheets and text entered in cells and fields.

ARIAL NARROW TEXT is used to denote the names of folders and files, and, when italicised, the names of worksheets in Excel workbooks.

Contents

Chapter 1: Introduction 1
   The case study 1
   The CD 1
   Before you start 2
      Copying files from the CD 3
      Turning off adaptive menus 3
   Online help 4

Chapter 2: Using templates in Excel 5
   In this chapter 5
      New skills 5
      New words 5
      Syllabus reference 5
   Creating spreadsheets from templates 6
      Creating an invoice from a template 7
      Over to you: optional 8
   Creating templates 9
   Editing templates 10
      Editing a template 10
      Over to you: optional 11
   Chapter summary 11
   Quick Quiz 12
      Answers 13

Chapter 3: Importing data into a spreadsheet 15
   In this chapter 15
      New skills 15
      New words 15
      Syllabus reference 16
   Importing data from an external source 16
   Importing data from text files 16
      Structured text files 16
      Text qualifiers 17
      Importing delimited text files 17
      Over to you: mandatory 21
   Querying a database from Excel 21
      Creating a simple query 22
      Over to you: mandatory 24

Using filter and sort in a database query 24
    Running a saved query 25
    Editing queries 26
    Over to you: mandatory 28
Advanced querying 29
    Filters in Microsoft Query 29
    Creating an advanced filter 30
    Over to you: mandatory 33
Chapter summary 33
Quick Quiz 34
    Answers 35

Chapter 4: Sorting data in a spreadsheet 37
In this chapter 37
    New skills 37
    New words 37
    Syllabus reference 37
Sorting data in Excel 38
    Sorting multiple columns at the same time 38
    Over to you: optional 39
Custom sort orders 40
    Using a custom sort order 40
Defining a custom list 42
    Over to you: optional 44
Chapter summary 44
Quick Quiz 44
    Answers 45

Chapter 5: Naming cells and adding comments 47
In this chapter 47
    New skills 47
    New words 47
    Syllabus reference 48
Cell names 48
    Custom cell names 48
    Custom cell names and formulae 49
    Assigning a custom name to a cell range 50
    Over to you: mandatory 51
Comments 51
    Adding comments 52
    Reading comments 52
    Editing comments 53
    Deleting comments 54

Chapter summary 54
Quick Quiz 55
    Answers 56

Chapter 6: Using Paste Special 57
In this chapter 57
    New skills 57
    New words 57
    Syllabus reference 57
Why Paste Special? 58
Pasting different types of information 59
The Operations area 62
Special options 63
    Skip blanks 63
    Transpose 64
    Paste Link 65
    Over to you: optional 66
Chapter summary 66
Quick Quiz 67
    Answers 68

Chapter 7: Summarizing data using PivotTables 69
In this chapter 69
    New skills 69
    New words 69
    Syllabus reference 69
What are PivotTables? 70
    Example of a PivotTable 70
    PivotTable layout 71
    Filtering using fields 72
Creating PivotTables 73
Grouping data in PivotTables 76
    Over to you: mandatory 79
Refresh PivotTables 80
    Over to you: optional 81
Chapter summary 81
Quick Quiz 82
    Answers 83

Chapter 8: Linking to data in spreadsheets 85
In this chapter 85
    New skills 85
    New words 85
    Syllabus reference 85

Linking to a cell on the same worksheet 86
Linking to cells in other worksheets 87
Linking to cells in other workbooks 88
Cell references in formulae 88
Linking to cells in Excel workbooks from Word 89
    Over to you: optional 91
Linking charts 91
Chapter summary 92
Quick Quiz 93
    Answers 94

Chapter 9: Formatting your spreadsheets 95
In this chapter 95
    New skills 95
    New words 95
    Syllabus reference 95
Freezing row and column titles 96
Using AutoFormat 98
    Over to you: optional 99
Custom number formats 99
Conditional formatting 102
    Over to you: optional 104
Chapter summary 104
Quick Quiz 105
    Answers 106

Chapter 10: Using Excel macros 107
In this chapter 107
    New skills 107
    New words 107
    Syllabus reference 107
What are macros? 108
Recording macros 109
    Absolute macros 109
    Relative macros 110
Running macros 112
Adding macros to a toolbar 113
    Over to you: optional 115
Chapter summary 115
Quick Quiz 115
    Answers 116

Chapter 11: Using reference and mathematical functions **117**
   In this chapter 117
      New skills 117
      New words 117
      Syllabus reference 117
   Maths with Paste Special 118
      Over to you: mandatory 119
   Reference functions 119
      VLOOKUP 120
      Over to you: mandatory 122
      HLOOKUP 123
   Subtotalling 124
      Over to you: mandatory 126
   3D sum 127
   SUMIF 128
      Over to you: optional 129
      SUMPOSITIVE 129
   ROUND 129
   Nesting 131
   Chapter summary 132
   Quick Quiz 133
      Answers 134

Chapter 12: Customising charts **135**
   In this chapter 135
      New skills 135
      New words 135
      Syllabus reference 135
   Deleting a data series from a chart 136
      Over to you: mandatory 138
   Modifying the chart type for a data series 139
      Over to you: mandatory 140
   Formatting chart axes 140
      Over to you: mandatory 141
   Widening the gaps between columns in a chart 141
   Inserting a picture in a chart 142
   Changing the angle of slices in a pie chart 144
   Exploding all the slices in a pie chart 147
   Repositioning chart elements 148
      Over to you: mandatory 148
   Chapter summary 149

Quick Quiz 149
    Answers 150

Chapter 13: Using statistical and database functions 151
In this chapter 151
    New skills 151
    New words 151
    Syllabus reference 151
Statistical functions 152
    COUNT 152
    COUNTA 153
    COUNTIF 154
Database functions 154
    DSUM 155
    DMIN 156
    DMAX 157
    DCOUNT 158
Chapter summary 159
Quick Quiz 159
    Answers 161

Chapter 14: Using financial functions 163
In this chapter 163
    New skills 163
    New words 163
    Syllabus reference 163
NPV 164
PV 166
FV 167
PMT 168
RATE 170
Chapter summary 171
Quick Quiz 172
    Answers 173

Chapter 15: Using text and date functions 175
In this chapter 175
    New skills 175
    New words 175
    Syllabus reference 175
Text functions 176
    PROPER 176

      UPPER 176
      LOWER 177
      Reusing text values in longer strings 177
      CONCATENATE 177
   Date 178
      TODAY 178
      DAY, MONTH and YEAR 179
   Chapter summary 179
   Quick Quiz 180
      Answers 181

Chapter 16: Using logical functions 183
   In this chapter 183
      New skills 183
      New words 183
      Syllabus reference 183
   IF 184
      Over to you: mandatory 185
   AND 185
   OR 187
      Over to you: mandatory 187
      Over to you: optional 188
   ISERROR 188
      Over to you: optional 189
   Chapter summary 189
   Quick Quiz 189
      Answers 190

Chapter 17: Using data tables and scenarios 191
   In this chapter 191
      New skills 191
      New words 191
      Syllabus reference 192
   Data tables 192
   1-input data tables 193
   2-input data tables 195
   Named scenarios 196
      Creating a scenario 197
      Over to you: mandatory 198
      Viewing a scenario 199
   Scenario summaries 199
   Chapter summary 200

Quick Quiz	201
Answers	202

Chapter 18: Auditing your spreadsheets 203

In this chapter	203
New skills	203
New words	203
Syllabus reference	203
Formulae and locations	204
Go To	204
Displaying formulae	205
Tracing precedent cells	206
Tracing dependent cells	207
Chapter summary	208
Quick Quiz	209
Answers	210

Chapter 19: Sharing and protecting your spreadsheets 211

In this chapter	211
New skills	211
New words	211
Syllabus reference	211
Hiding columns and rows	212
Hiding a column	212
Unhiding a column	213
Hiding and unhiding rows	213
Hiding worksheets	213
Unhiding worksheets	214
Protecting cells	215
Specifying protection settings for a cell	215
Protecting worksheets	216
Protecting workbooks	218
Chapter summary	219
Quick Quiz	219
Answers	220

In conclusion 221

Appendix: Advanced spreadsheets test 223

In this section	223
The test	223

Index 227

Chapter 1: Introduction

The case study

The exercises in this book relate to the spreadsheets used by the fictitious company, Murphy's Flatpack Furniture, or MFPF.

MFPF is a family-run business, producing a range of flatpack furniture. The current range includes five indoor pieces (bed, wardrobe, chest of drawers, coffee table and kitchen organizer), and two outdoor pieces (garden chair and garden table).

MFPF sells furniture to six retailers: three in Cullenstown, where MFPF is based, and three in neighbouring villages.

Mr and Mrs Murphy are not salaried, but they retain any profits made by the business. Their daughter works in the warehouse and receives a monthly salary.

Regular business expenses are materials, warehouse rental, petrol, electricity and telephone.

You have just been hired as a bookkeeper for the business. Your duties include looking after invoices, maintaining records on the financial transactions of the business, and producing reports, summaries and forecasts when requested.

The CD

The CD supplied with this book contains the following files:

- DELIVERY_COSTS.TXT – a delimited text file that lists the road distance to each customer and the delivery charge applied to their orders.
- INVOICE_MFPF.XLT – an Excel template for sales invoices.
- LETTER.DOC – the start of a letter to the local bank manager in relation to a business loan.
- LOGO.GIF – MFPF's company logo.

- MFPF_FINANCE.XLS – the start of a spreadsheet used to track the business's annual incomings, outgoings and profits.
- MFPF_ORD.MDB – an Access database containing details of MFPF's customers and all the orders they placed in 2000.
- OUTGOING.TXT – a delimited text file that lists the monthly cost of regular business expenses.
- PASTE_SPECIAL.XLS – a spreadsheet containing an assortment of miscellaneous information.
- PRICES.TXT – a delimited text file listing the costs of materials for each furniture type produced, and the price at which the finished products are sold.

You will use these files when completing the exercises in the book.

In addition:

- The worked exercises folder contains the *resulting* spreadsheets for the numbered exercises in the book and the mandatory *Over to you* exercises named according to the exercise that generates them.
  For example, Ex3.1-MFPF_FINANCE.xls shows how the MFPF_FINANCE.xls file should appear once you have completed Exercise 3.1; Ex3.1-OTYM1-MFPF_FINANCE.xls shows how MFPF_FINANCE.xls should appear once you have completed the first mandatory *Over to you* exercise after Exercise 3.1.
  At the start of each exercise, you will have the option of using your own files or specific files from the CD as a starting point, and after each exercise you can check your own results against those on the CD.
- The test folder contains two spreadsheets for use when completing the sample test at the end of the book.

Before you start

Before you begin working through the exercises in this book, you will need to copy the files from the CD to your computer.

Copying files from the CD

In the following exercise you will copy the INVOICE_MFPF.XLT template to Excel's templates folder, then create a working folder to which you will copy the remainder of the files from the CD.

Note: If you want to, you can copy the worked exercises from the CD to your hard disk for easy access, but if you're running low on free space you can access these files from the CD if and when you need to instead.

Exercise 1.1: Copying files from the CD to your computer

1. Copy the Excel template INVOICE_MFPF.XLT from the CD to the following folder:
   [...]\Application Data\Microsoft\Templates
   Where this folder is located will depend on your operating system.
   You can locate the folder by searching for the file Normal.dot, the default Word template which is located in this folder.

   Note: In order to see the Templates folder, you must be able to see hidden files and folders in Windows Explorer. To turn this option on, if it is not already enabled:
   - Open Windows Explorer.
   - Click **Tools | Folder Options...**.
   - Go to the **View** tab of the *Folder Options* dialog box.
   - Select *Show hidden files and folders* in the *Advanced settings* area.
   - Click **Apply to all folders**.
2. Create a folder called ECDL_EXCEL anywhere on your computer.
   This will be your working folder for the exercises in this book.
3. Copy the other files from the disk to the ECDL_EXCEL folder. Remember that you do not need to copy the contents of the worked exercises folder unless you want to.

Turning off adaptive menus

Excel's adaptive menus show the commands you have used most recently first. Since the exercises in this book cover advanced Excel features, many require less commonly used commands, so you may find it convenient to turn off adaptive menus before you start.

Exercise 1.2: How to turn off adaptive menus

1. Start Excel.
2. Select **View | Toolbars | Customize...**.
   The *Customize* dialog box opens.
3. Click the **Options** tab.
4. Check the box beside *Always show full menus* and click **Close**.

Online help

This text guides you through how to perform each of the tasks on the ECDL Advanced Spreadsheets syllabus using Excel.

When you take your ECDL Advanced Spreadsheets exam, however, you won't be able to take this book with you – *but*, as with the ECDL 3 or ECDL 4 exam, you *will* be allowed to use Microsoft Office's online help during the ECDL Advanced Exam.

You can access the online help quickly by pressing the **F1** key on your keyboard – otherwise click **Help | Microsoft Excel Help** (**Help | Microsoft Office Excel Help** in Excel 2003).

Take some time before the exam to familiarize yourself with the available help topics on any area(s) of this syllabus you find particularly difficult so that you know what to look for when you're under pressure and time is short.

Chapter 2: Using templates in Excel

In this chapter

Every time you create a new spreadsheet in Excel, you base it on a template.

In this chapter you will learn about templates in Excel: what they are, what information they contain, and how to use them. You will also learn how to edit templates, and how to create templates of your own.

New skills

At the end of this chapter you should be able to:

- Explain what a template is
- Explain why you would want to use a template
- Give examples of the types of information that can be stored in a template
- Find Excel templates on your PC
- Create spreadsheets from templates
- Create and edit templates

New words

At the end of this chapter you should be able to explain the following terms:
- Template
- Boilerplate text

Syllabus reference

The following syllabus items are covered in this chapter:
- AM 4.2.4.1 – Use a template.
- AM 4.2.4.2 – Edit a template.

Creating spreadsheets from templates

Every time you create a new spreadsheet in Excel, you use a template that defines the default settings and content for the spreadsheet.

> **Template**
>
> *In Excel, a template is a type of spreadsheet that contains default information and settings, and is used to create new spreadsheets with the same look and feel.*
> *Excel templates have the file extension .xlt.*

Even the 'empty' workbook that opens by default when you start Excel is based on a template. The template contains no text or numeric data, but it does have default layout and style content.

Start Excel and have a closer look at the default workbook that opens.

Normally, the default workbook contains 3 worksheets. (The default may have been changed on your computer.) Each worksheet has 256 columns and 65,536 rows. Every column has a standard width; every row has a standard height. The font in every cell is Arial 10pt. All of this is defined by the default template.

Most templates you use in Excel contain default text, such as row and column labels, which is included in every new spreadsheet generated from the template. This text is known as boilerplate text.

> **Boilerplate text**
>
> *Default text included in a template is called boilerplate text. It is added to every spreadsheet created from that template.*

Templates can also contain layout and style formatting, numbers, formulae, macros, charts and any other type of information or setting that can be added to a spreadsheet in Excel.

Using a template to generate a particular type of spreadsheet that you use regularly can save you a lot of time and effort. Only the case-specific data will need to be added each time.

Creating an invoice from a template

Mr Murphy has given you your first task for Murphy's Flatpack Furniture. He wants you to issue an invoice to a customer, using Excel. The invoice should indicate who has issued it and when, who it was issued to, what goods were ordered and how much they cost. MFPF will keep an electronic copy of the invoice for its own records, and print out a copy to send to the customer.

To create the invoice, you could start with the default workbook and add labels and numbers for the required details, and then apply formatting before printing it and sending it to the customer. Fortunately, though, there's an invoice template available with all the default information already there.

> **Note:** If you didn't complete *Exercise 1.1* on page 3 you should go back and do it now. The exercises use files supplied on the disk that comes with the book. These files must be in specific locations before you start.

Exercise 2.1: Creating a spreadsheet from a template

1. Start Excel, if it is not already open.
2. Select **File | New...** to open the *New Workbook* task pane. This task pane allows you to choose to open an existing workbook, open a new blank workbook, create a new workbook based on an existing workbook, or create a new workbook from a template.
3. In Excel XP, the task pane shows a *New from template* area: click **General Templates...** in this area to open the *Templates* dialog box.
   In Excel 2003, the task pane shows a *Templates* area: in this area, click *On my computer* to open the *Templates* dialog box.
4. Click the **General** tab of the *Templates* dialog box.

A list of available templates is shown.

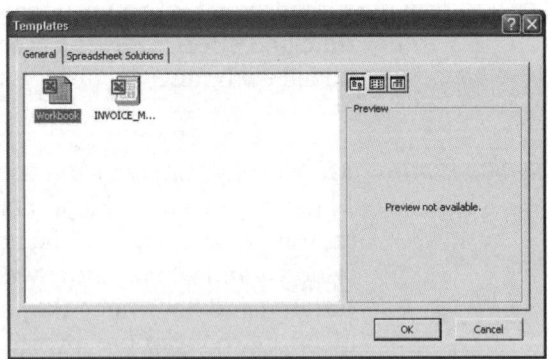

5. Select *INVOICE_MFPF.XLT* and click **OK**.
   A new spreadsheet opens.
   This spreadsheet contains all the default information and settings defined by the template.
   To write an invoice, you just need to fill in the blanks.

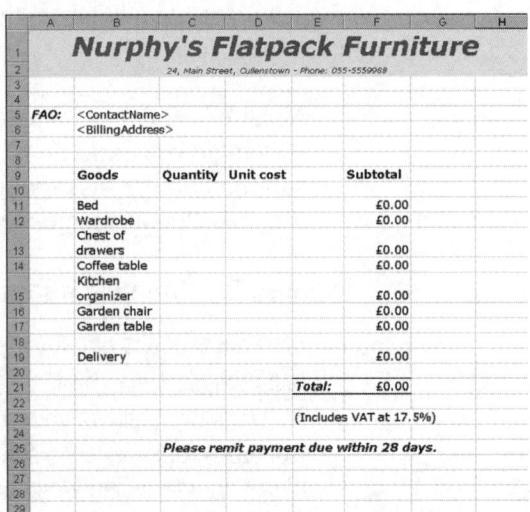

Save button

6. Select **File | Save**, or click the **Save** button on the *Standard* toolbar.
   The *Save As* dialog box opens.
7. Name the spreadsheet INVOICE1.XLS, and save it in your working folder, ECDL_EXCEL.

Over to you: optional

Next, you will look at some more templates.

Open the *Templates* dialog box by clicking **General Templates...** under *New from template* in the Excel XP task pane, or by clicking **On my computer** under *Templates* in the Excel 2003 task pane.

The *Templates* dialog box lists all of the templates available on your computer. The **Spreadsheet Solutions** tab contains templates which have been provided by Microsoft. All other templates are shown on the **General** tab. *Workbook* is the default template we saw earlier.

- Open the other Excel templates on your computer and see what information and settings they contain. Try to think of other spreadsheet templates you might find useful.

Creating templates

You can create a new template by adding the default information and settings you want in the template to a spreadsheet, and then saving the spreadsheet as a template using **File | Save as...**.

When you save a spreadsheet as a template, Excel automatically changes the file extension to .XLT and opens the correct folder for saving Excel templates. This is the easiest way to locate the correct folder for Excel templates on your machine.

Alternatively, you can add templates to the **General** tab of the *New* dialog box by putting Excel template files in one of the following folders:

- <Drive>:\PROGRAM FILES\MICROSOFT OFFICE\OFFICE10\XLSTART for Excel XP
  or
  <Drive>:\PROGRAM FILES\MICROSOFT OFFICE\OFFICE11\XLSTART for Excel 2003
  where <Drive> is the drive on which Excel was installed, e.g. C or D.
- [...]\APPLICATION DATA\MICROSOFT\TEMPLATES
  Where this folder is located will depend on your operating system.

Editing templates

There are two ways to edit an existing template:
- Select **File | Open...**, locate the template, edit it directly, and save your results.
  – or –
- Select **File | New...**, create a new spreadsheet based on the template, make changes to the spreadsheet, then save it as a template, using the name of the existing template.

The second option is preferable, because if you decide at any point that you are not happy with your changes, you still have the original template and have not lost any work.

Editing a template

There are some problems with the invoice template you used earlier. There is a typo in the company name on the first page, and despite a request that the invoice be paid within 28 days there is nowhere to indicate on what date it was issued!

In the following exercise, you will create a spreadsheet from the invoice template, edit the spreadsheet to fix these problems and make some other formatting changes, and then save it as a template, replacing the original INVOICE_MFPF.XLT.

Exercise 2.2: Editing a template

1. Create a new spreadsheet based on the invoice template.
2. Select **File | Save**, or click the **Save** button on the *Standard* toolbar.
3. Name your file INVOICE_MFPF.XLS and save it in the ECDL_EXCEL folder.
4. Make the following changes to the spreadsheet:
   - On the **Customer Invoice** worksheet, fix the typo in the spelling of *Murphy*.
   - Increase the font size for the invoice total in cell *F21* to 12 point.
   - Decrease the font size of the list of goods in cell range *B11:B19* to 10 point.

- The invoice should be paid within 28 days, but the issue date is not indicated anywhere. Enter the label *Date:* in cell *E5*, and format it as bold italic.
5. Save your workbook when you are done.
6. Select **File | Save as...**, and select *Template (*.xlt)* from the *Save as type* drop-down list.
Excel changes the file extension and automatically opens the TEMPLATES folder.
7. Select the existing *INVOICE_MFPF.XLT* to replace it, and click **Save**.
A dialog box appears, asking you to confirm that you want to replace the existing *INVOICE_MFPF.XLT*.
8. Click **Yes**.

Congratulations! You just saved your first template! Just think about how much time and energy you will save in the future when you have created templates for all of the spreadsheets you regularly use.

Over to you: optional

To see that your changes are now part of the invoice template, you will create a new spreadsheet based on the template.

- Create a new spreadsheet based on INVOICE_MFPF.XLT. See that the changes you made in *Exercise 2.2* on page 10 are now part of the default information in the template. Close Excel when you are finished.

Chapter summary

In Excel, a template is a type of spreadsheet that contains default information and settings, and is used to create new spreadsheets with the same look and feel. Excel templates have the file extension .xlt.

Templates can contain any type of information or setting that can be added to a spreadsheet in Excel, including text, graphics, layout and style formatting, numbers, formulae, macros and charts.

Default text included in a template is called boilerplate text. It is added to every spreadsheet created from that template.

Quick Quiz

Circle the answer to each of the following multiple-choice questions about Excel templates.

Q1	An Excel template can include...
A.	Embedded graphics.
B.	Text and numeric data.
C.	Font and colour information.
D.	All of the above.

Q2	Boilerplate text is...
A.	Operating instructions printed on a water boiler.
B.	Default text included in a template.
C.	Any text in a spreadsheet using the Boilerplate font.
D.	Text that appears in the header/footer of a spreadsheet when you print it.

Q3	Excel templates have the extension...
A.	.XLT
B.	.XTL
C.	.XLS
D.	.XTM

Q4	An Excel template *must* include at least one formula.
A.	True.
B.	False.

Q5	An Excel template must have at least three worksheets.
A.	True.
B.	False.

Q6	Excel templates cannot be edited directly.
A.	True.
B.	False.

Answers   **1:** D; **2:** B; **3:** A; **4:** B; **5:** B; **6:** B.

Chapter 3: Importing data into a spreadsheet

In this chapter

From time to time, you may find that you want to reuse some or all of the data from another source in an Excel spreadsheet.

For example, you might want to reuse a list of staff members from a telephone list as row labels in a worksheet where you will calculate your annual salary budget. Or you might want to include petty cash records from a database in your expenses calculations.

Excel's data import facility allows you to import all or part of the data in a *delimited* text file (one where 'columns' of data are separated by specific characters) or a database into a spreadsheet. In this chapter you will learn how to import data from delimited text files and from an Access database into Excel.

New skills

At the end of this chapter you should be able to:

- Import data from delimited text files
- Import data from a database using a query
- Run a saved database query
- Edit a database query
- Add filter and sort requirements to a database query

New words

At the end of this chapter you should be able to explain the following terms:

- Delimited text file
- Text qualifier
- Query
- Criteria
- Filter

Syllabus reference

The following syllabus items are covered in this chapter:
- AM 4.1.1.6 – Import a text file and delimit by comma, space or tab.
- AM 4.2.2.1 – Create a single or multiple criteria query using available options.
- AM 4.2.2.2 – Use advanced query / filter options.

Importing data from an external source

In ECDL 3 or ECDL 4 you imported objects created in other programs into Excel spreadsheets. These objects included images and text files.

You can also choose to import textual data from an external source and include them in the cells of an Excel spreadsheet. These data can then be formatted, manipulated and used in formulae, just like any other data in Excel.

When you import data from an external source, Excel remembers which file or database you imported your data from, and the setting you used to import it. If the data in the source file change, you can update the imported data in Excel by selecting the imported data, and selecting **Data | Refresh Data** or by clicking the **Refresh Data** button on the *External Data* toolbar.

Refresh Data button

If you cannot see the *External Data* toolbar, you can turn it on by selecting **View | Toolbars | External Data**.

Importing data from text files

When you import data from a text file, the text file will usually be formatted in rows and columns. You can use Excel's *Text Import Wizard* to specify how the data have been formatted, so that you can preserve the row and column structure when you import the data into Excel.

Structured text files

When importing structured text files, Excel treats each new line as a row. Excel recognizes two different ways that columns can be represented:

- The columns can be *delimited*, which means that a particular character or set of characters is used to indicate where one column stops and the next begins.
- The columns can be structured with a *fixed width*, which means that a number of tabs, spaces, or a combination of the two is used to make all the entries in a column line up.

> **Delimited text file**
>
> *A text file in which columns of information are separated from each other by a particular character or set of characters is known as a delimited text file.*

Text qualifiers

If any of the data elements in your delimited text file contain the character that has been used as a delimiter, you can use a text qualifier to mark the beginning and end of the data element. The *Text Import Wizard* ignores any delimiter characters that appear between a pair of text qualifiers.

> **Text qualifier**
>
> *A character used to mark the beginning and end of a data element in a delimited text file. Usually, single or double quotation marks are used as text qualifiers.*

For example, if you were using a space as a delimiter, Excel would parse the following record as containing five columns
Cullenstown Garden Centre 2 5

But by introducing a double quotation mark as a text qualifier, you can get Excel to ignore the first two spaces and parse the record correctly as containing three columns:
"*Cullenstown Garden Centre*" *2 5*

Importing delimited text files

Mrs Murphy has asked you to import data about MFPF's business expenses from three delimited text files into two spreadsheets, where the data can be used in calculations of monthly running costs.

The three files are:

- OUTGOING.TXT, which is space-delimited and shows the regular expenses incurred by the business every month.
- PRICES.TXT, which is tab-delimited and shows the cost of the materials for each type of furniture produced by the business, and the wholesale price for which they are sold.
- DELIVERY_COSTS.TXT, which is comma-delimited and shows the distance to each customer's premises, and the delivery charge for each order.

Each file uses double quotation marks as text qualifiers.

In the next exercise you will import the first of these files into the MFPF_FINANCE.XLS spreadsheet.

Exercise 3.1: Importing a space-delimited text file

1. Open the spreadsheet MFPF_FINANCE.XLS.
2. Select **Data | Import External Data | Import Data...**.
   The *Select Data Source File* dialog box opens.

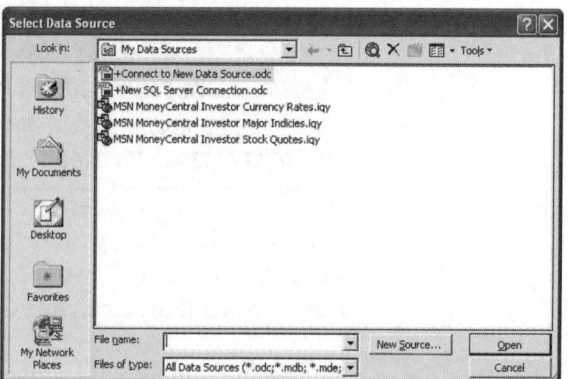

3. From the *Files of type* drop-down list, select *Text files*, then browse to and select OUTGOING.TXT in your working folder and click **Open**.
   The *Text Import Wizard* opens.
4. Indicate that your data are *Delimited*, and that you want to *Start import at row 1*.
   Click **Next**.

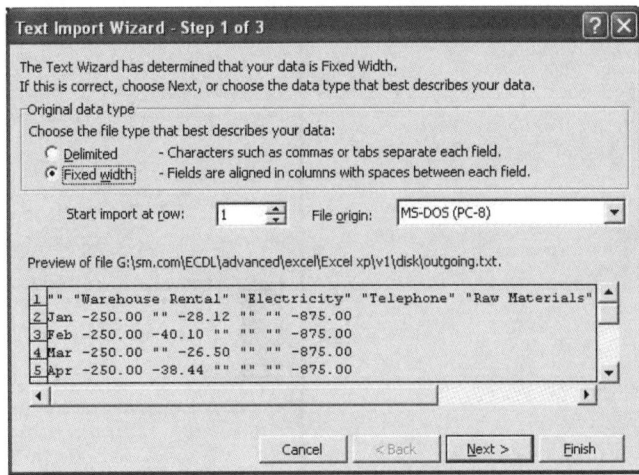

5. The file you are importing is space-delimited, so in the *Delimiters* area on the dialog box that now appears, check the box beside *Space* and uncheck the one beside *Tab*.
   If you used a mixture of spaces *and* tabs as delimiters in the source text file, you would check both the *Space* and *Tab* boxes here, and so on for any other delimiters used. Mixing delimiters isn't generally a very good idea, though, as you may find it difficult to read your own data again later!

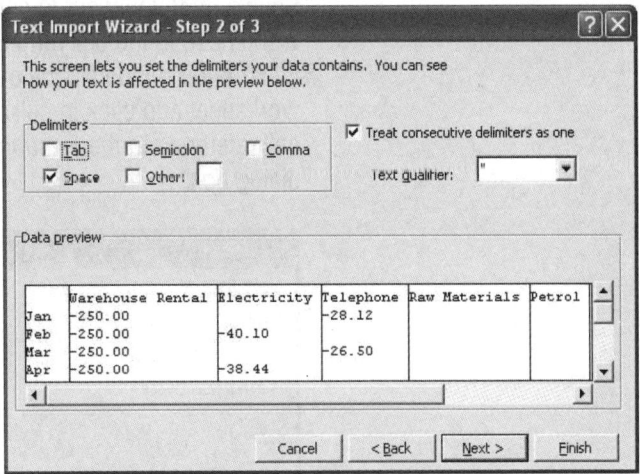

In the *Text qualifier* field, select the double quotation mark. Click **Next**.

6. In the *Column data format* area you can specify a format for the column selected in the *Data preview* area, or select *Do not import column* to skip the column when importing.

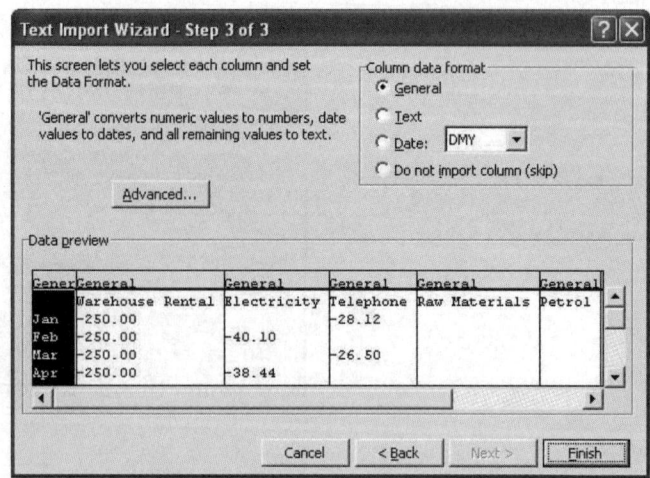

To select a column, click anywhere in the column in the *Data preview* area of the dialog box, then select the appropriate *Column Data Format*. The heading of the column changes to indicate which data format has been applied.

In this case, you will import all the columns with a *General* format, which is the default.

Click **Finish**.

The *Import Data* dialog box opens.

7. Specify that you want to add the data to the *OUTGOING* worksheet, in the cell range starting in cell *A1*.

   Either enter the details below manually, or open the *OUTGOING* worksheet and click in cell *A1* to automatically add the correct cell reference to the *Existing worksheet* field of the *Import Data* dialog box.

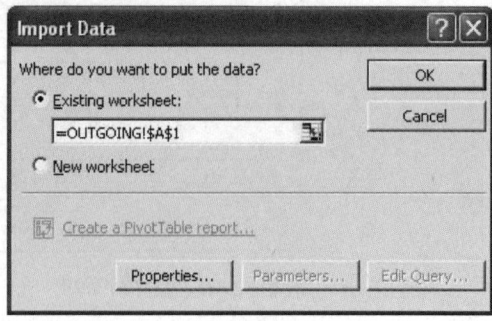

Click **OK**.

The data from the text file are added to the *OUTGOING* worksheet.

8. Save your workbook.

Well done! You have just imported a year's worth of expenses information from a space-delimited text file into a spreadsheet in a matter of minutes.

Over to you: mandatory

Next, you will import the other two delimited text files into other worksheets.

- Import the data from PRICES.TXT into MFPF_FINANCE.XLS (or Ex3.1-MFPF_FINANCE.xls). Add the data in a cell range starting at cell *A15* on the *SALES TOTALS* worksheet. The first row in PRICES.TXT contains the column titles already present on this worksheet, so you do not need to include them: start your import at row *2*. Import all columns with a general format. When you are done, save and close the workbook.
- Create a new workbook called DELIVERIES.XLS based on the default template. Rename one of the worksheets *CHARGES* and import DELIVERY_COSTS.TXT into it. When you are done, save and close the workbook.

You should be able to tell what type of delimiter was used in each file either by opening the file and examining it, or by trying the different options in the *Text Import Wizard* until you find which one(s) make the data line up in a sensible way.

Querying a database from Excel

You have successfully imported data from a variety of delimited text files. Next, you will learn how to import data from a database.

To import data from a database, you create a query that specifies the information you want. Then you run the query, and put the results in your Excel spreadsheet.

> **Query**
>
> *A query is a set of rules that say what records, or parts of records, to retrieve from a database, and how to display those data.*

Creating a simple query

The Access database MFPF_ORD.MDB contains contact information for each of Murphy's Flatpack Furniture's customers, and details of their orders for the last year.

You have been asked to import from the database only those columns that indicate the date of an order, the company that made the order, the town it is based in, and how many units of each type of furniture it ordered.

In the next exercise you will create a simple query to import the specified columns from MFPF_ORD.MDB. You will also save the query you create so that you can run it again later.

> **Note:** If Microsoft Query is not installed on your machine, you will be prompted to install it when you first try to create a database query.

Exercise 3.2: Creating a simple database query in Excel

1. Create a new workbook called MFPF_ORD.XLS, based on the default template, and rename the first worksheet *COMPLETE*.

2. Select **Data | Import External Data | New Database Query...**.
   The *Choose Data Source* dialog box opens.

   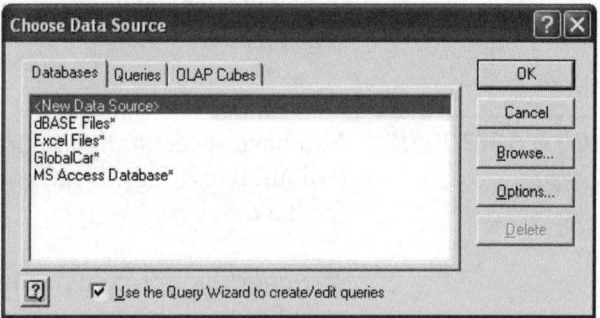

3. Select *MS Access Database** from the list of databases.
   Make sure the box beside *Use the Query Wizard to create/edit queries* is checked, then click **OK**.
   The *Select Database* dialog box opens.

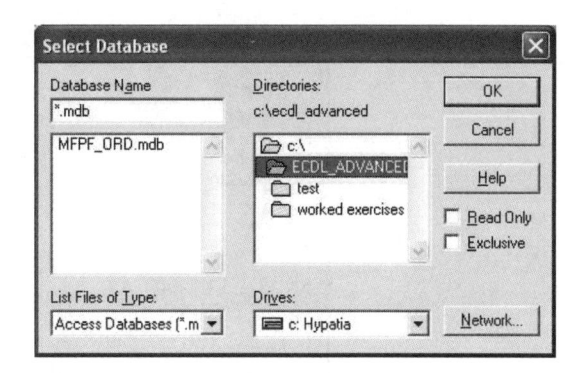

4. Select the MFPF_ORD.MDB database in your working folder. If the drive on which your working folder is not selected by default in the *Drives* drop-down list, you will need to select the correct drive from this list first.
   Click **OK**.
   The *Query Wizard – Choose Columns* dialog box opens.

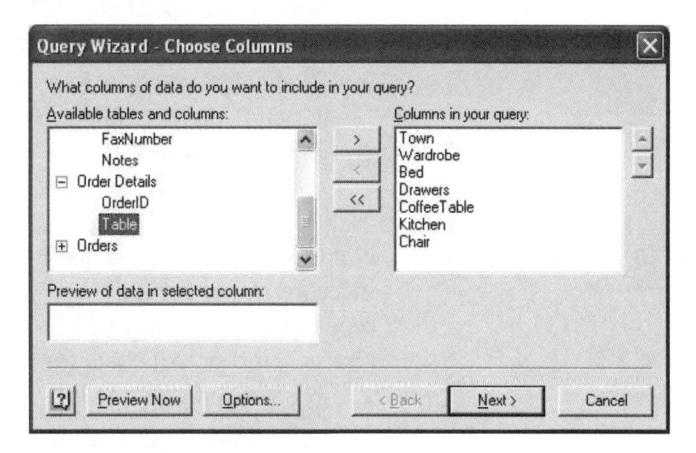

5. Select the following columns in this order:
   - From the *Orders* table: *OrderDate*
   - From the *Customers* table: *CompanyName* and *Town*
   - From the *Order Details* table: *Wardrobe*, *Bed*, *Drawers*, *CoffeeTable*, *Kitchen*, *Chair* and *Table*

   Keep clicking **Next** until you get to the *Query Wizard – Finish* dialog box.

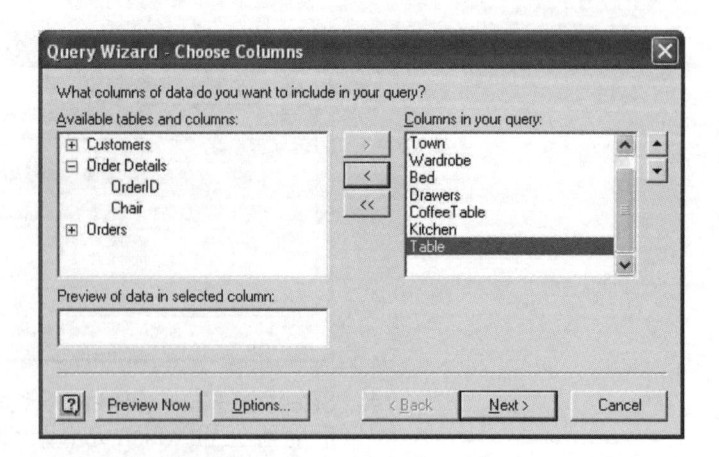

6. Click **Save Query...**.
   The *Save As* dialog box opens.
7. Name the query *MFPF_Q1.DQY* and click **Save**.
8. Select *Return Data to Microsoft Excel* and click **Finish**.
   The *Import Data* dialog box opens.
9. Specify that you want to put the data in the cell range beginning in cell *A1* on the *COMPLETE* worksheet, and click **OK**.
10. Save your workbook.

Over to you: mandatory

Next, you will create a query to retrieve the columns that indicate the order date and company name for each order placed. These details will be used later to calculate delivery charges and petrol costs for each order.

- Open DELIVERIES.XLS (or Ex3.1-OTYM2-DELIVERIES.xls) and create a query that retrieves from MFPF_ORD.MDB the following columns (in order): *DeliveryDate* and *CompanyName* from the *Orders* table. Add the results to a new worksheet. Name the new worksheet *Deliveries*.

When you are done, save and close the workbook.

Using filter and sort in a database query

When you import data from delimited text files, you choose which columns to include, and at which row to start the import.

When you import data from a database, you have much more control over which rows (or records) to include. You can specify a set of criteria that the records you import should satisfy.

> **Criteria**
>
> *Criteria are rules that specify what records are imported, based on the value in a particular field.*

For example, you could use criteria to indicate that the value in a particular field must exactly match a specified value.

Criteria are combined together to create a filter.

> **Filter**
>
> *A filter limits the records imported from a database to those that satisfy specific criteria.*

You can even sort the records before importing them into your spreadsheet.

Running a saved query

Mrs Murphy has asked you to add two more worksheets to the MFPF_ORD.XLS workbook. The first should show order details for outdoor furniture (garden chairs and garden tables). The second should show details for indoor furniture (bed, wardrobe, chest of drawers, coffee table and kitchen organizer).

Additionally, she only wants to see the records for sales to customers in Cullenstown on each of these sheets.

In the next exercise, you will run the query you saved earlier to import order records into a new worksheet.

Exercise 3.3: Running a saved query

1. Open MFPF_ORD.XLS (or Ex3.2-MFPF_ORD.xls), and name one of the empty worksheets *INDOOR*.
2. Select **Data | Import External Data | Import Data...**.
   The *Select Data Source* dialog box opens.

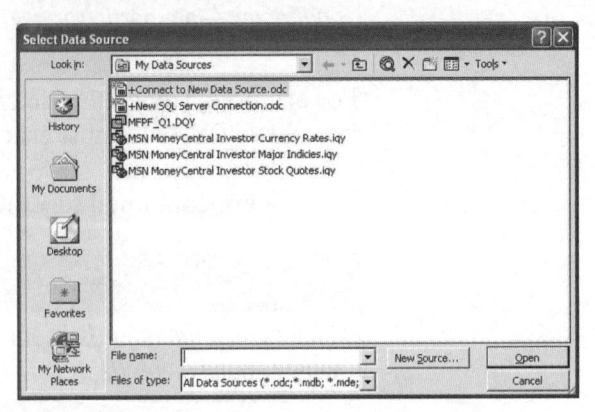

3. Select *MFPF_Q1.DQY* (the query you saved earlier – or use Ex3.2-MFPF_Q1.dqy from the CD) and click **Open**.
   The *Import Data* dialog box opens.
4. Specify that you want to put the data in the cell range beginning in cell *A1* on the *INDOOR* worksheet and click **OK**.
5. Save your workbook.

The *INDOOR* worksheet now contains the same information you imported into the *COMPLETE* worksheet when you first created and ran the MFPF_Q1.DQY query.

Editing queries

In the next exercise, you will edit the query to import information about sales of indoor furniture only. You will also add a filter so that only records relating to customers in Cullenstown are imported. Finally, just to make the results easier to read, you will sort the records in reverse chronological order, so that the most recent orders appear first.

> **Note:** You will not save the changes you make to the query, so the next time you run it, the results will be unfiltered and unsorted, as before.

Edit Query... button

Exercise 3.4: Editing a query

1. Open MFPF_ORD.XLS (or Ex3.3-MFPF_ORD.xls), and go to the *INDOOR* worksheet.

2. Select any cell in the range that contains the imported data, for example *A1*, and select **Data | Import External Data | Edit Query...**, or click the **Edit Query...** button on the *External Data* toolbar.
   If you cannot see the *External Data* toolbar, open it by selecting **View | Toolbars | External Data**.

3. Remove the columns for the sales of *Chairs* and *Tables*.

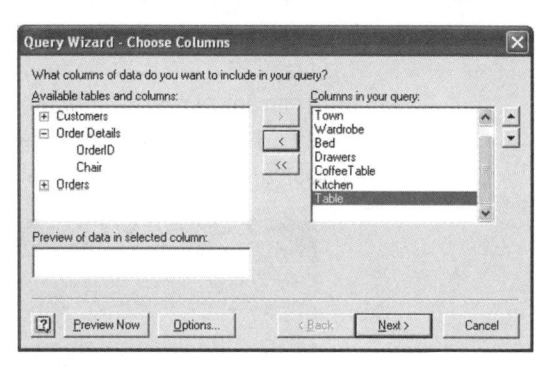

   Click **Next**.
   The *Query Wizard – Filter Data* dialog box opens.

4. In this dialog box, you will create a filter to limit the records returned by the query to those related to orders from customers in Cullenstown.
   In the *Only include rows where* area, select *Town* in the *Column to filter* list box, then select *equals* and *Cullenstown* from the drop-down lists of options.
   This is a criterion in your filter.

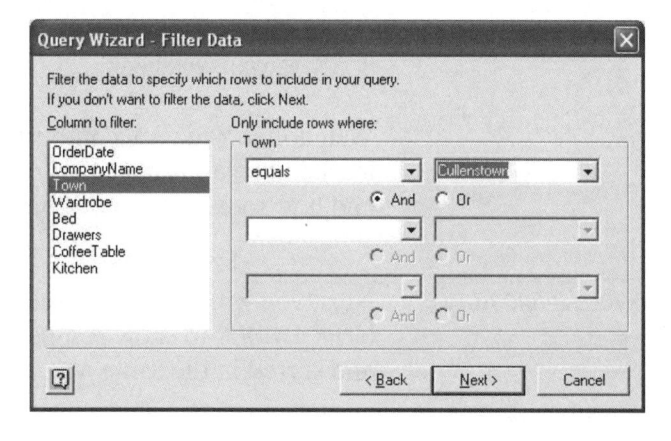

ECDL Advanced Spreadsheets for Microsoft® Office XP and 2003

You could add any number of other criteria to *Town* and other columns in this dialog box, if you wanted to.

You can combine the criteria for a single column using either logical AND or logical OR.

The filter requirements for different *columns*, however, are *always* combined using logical AND when specified through this dialog box. This means that for a record to get through the filter, it should satisfy the filter requirements you set for *each and every* column.

5. Click **Next**.
   The *Query Wizard – Sort Order* dialog box opens.
6. Sort by *OrderDate Descending* to see the most recent sales first.
   Then select *CompanyName Ascending*, so that if more than one sale was made on the same date, the sales for that date will be listed alphabetically by customer.

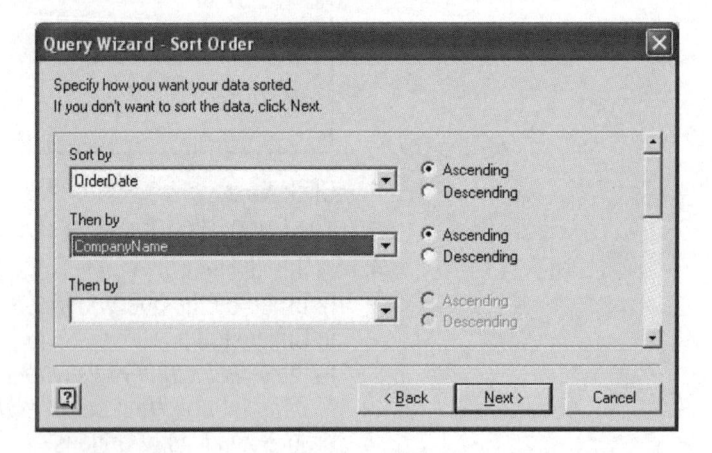

   Click **Next**.
7. Select *Return Data to Microsoft Excel* and click **Finish**.
8. Save your workbook.

Well done! You've accomplished a lot this time. You have learned how to run a saved query, how to edit that query, and how to use filter and sort when querying.

Over to you: mandatory

Next, you will filter the results from the saved query MFPF_Q1.DQY to show results for outdoor furniture, filtered and sorted in the same way.

28 Chapter 3: Importing data into a spreadsheet

- In the MFPF_ORD.XLS (or Ex3.4-MFPF_ORD.xls) workbook, create a worksheet called *OUTDOOR*.
- Run the saved query MFPF_Q1.DQY (or use Ex3.2-MFPF_Q1.dqy from the CD) and put the results on the *OUTDOOR* worksheet, starting in cell *A1*.
- Edit the query to show records for outdoor furniture (chairs and tables) sold in Cullenstown only, sorted in reverse chronological order.
- Save your workbook.

Advanced querying

Looking at the query results on the *INDOOR* and *OUTDOOR* worksheets, you can see that there are rows where none of the specified types of furniture were sold. These records are not really of any interest, but there is no way to filter them out using the *Query Wizard*.

Although you can combine the criteria for a given column using logical AND *or* logical OR, the sets of criteria for different columns are always combined using logical AND in the *Query Wizard*.

For example, you could create a filter to find orders where one or more pieces of furniture of a particular type was ordered (e.g. one or more chairs), but not one where one or more of *any* furniture type (e.g. one or more chairs *OR* one or more tables *OR* one or more wardrobes etc.) was ordered. To do that, you would need to be able to combine column filters using logical OR.

You can edit your query in Microsoft Query, instead of in the *Query Wizard*, to set more complex filters, using both logical AND and logical OR to combine all of your criteria, regardless of which columns they refer to.

Filters in Microsoft Query

In Microsoft Query, criteria are combined using logical AND and logical OR to create a set of distinct filter requirements.

Here is an example of how a set of filter requirements is represented in Microsoft Query:

Criteria Field:	CompanyName	Bed	CoffeeTable	
Value:	'Joe''s Hardware'	>0		
or:	'Mullens'		>1	

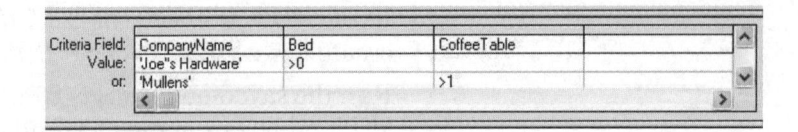

Criteria consist of *Criteria Fields* and *Values*. If a *Value* cell is left blank, then *any* value for the corresponding *Criteria Fields* are acceptable.

Each row represents a single filter requirement, where the criteria in the row are combined using logical AND.

The individual rows are combined using logical OR.

So, for a record to get through the filter, it must satisfy *all* of the criteria in *any* row.

In the example shown, a record will get through the filter if it is an order from *Joe's Hardware* AND at least one *Bed* was ordered, OR if it is an order from *Mullens* AND at least two *Coffee Tables* were ordered. No other records will get through.

Before you start to define a filter in Microsoft Query, you should be clear *exactly* what your filter requirements are, and how they relate to each other.

Creating an advanced filter

You want to filter out the records on the *INDOOR* and *OUTDOOR* worksheets of MFPF_ORD.XLS where no furniture was ordered. Remember that Mrs Murphy asked only to see records for customers in Cullenstown!

The individual filter requirements (rows) you will need to create are:

- The customer is from Cullenstown AND at least one bed was ordered
  OR
- The customer is from Cullenstown AND at least one wardrobe was ordered
  OR
- etc.

In the next exercise, you will use Microsoft Query to create an advanced query filter which finds records where at least one piece of indoor furniture was ordered by a shop in Cullenstown.

Exercise 3.5: Using advanced filtering in Microsoft Query

1. Open MFPF_ORD.XLS (or Ex3.4-OTYM1-MFPF_ORD.xls) and go to the *INDOOR* worksheet.
2. Select any cell in the query results, and select **Data | Import External Data | Edit Query...**, or click the **Edit Query...** button on the *External Data* toolbar.
   The *Query Wizard* opens.
3. Click **Cancel**.
   A dialog box opens asking you if you would like to continue editing the query in Microsoft Query.
4. Click **Yes**.
   Microsoft Query opens.

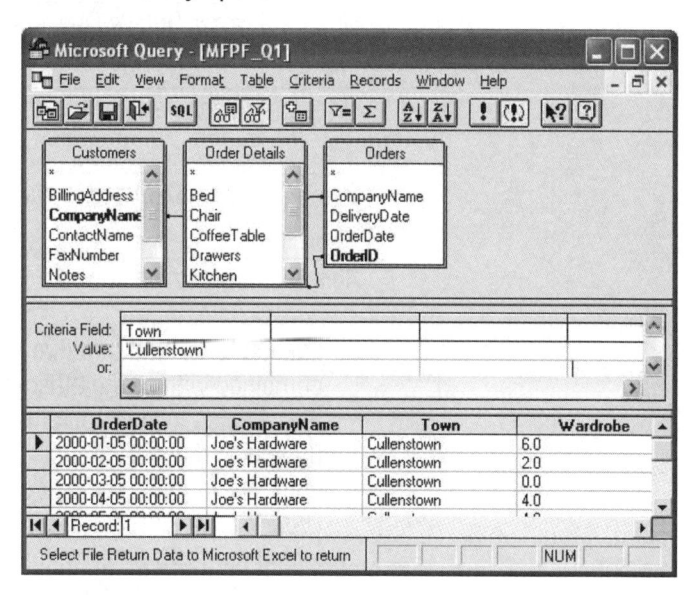

5. Select **Criteria | Remove All Criteria** to delete the filter you set earlier for the *Town* column area, before you add new filter rules.
6. You could add your criteria by typing directly in the *Criteria Field* and *Value* cells, but instead you will use the *Add Criteria* dialog box.
   Select **Criteria | Add Criteria...**.
   The *Add Criteria* dialog box appears.

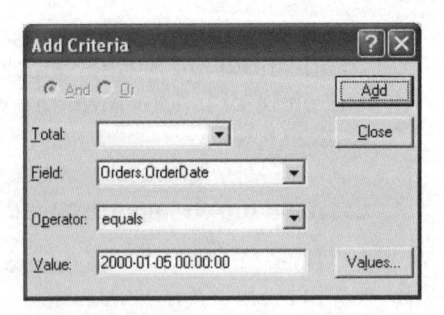

```
Add Criteria                    [?][X]
   (•) And  ( ) Or                [ Add  ]
Total:   [           |v]          [ Close ]
Field:   [Orders.OrderDate    |v]
Operator: [equals              |v]
Value:   [2000-01-05 00:00:00]    [Values...]
```

7. Add the following criteria to your filter in order, clicking **Add** after specifying each one:

And/Or	Field	Operator	Value
	Order Details.Bed	*Is greater than*	*0*
Or	*Order Details.CoffeeTable*	*Is greater than*	*0*
Or	*Order Details.Drawers*	*Is greater than*	*0*
Or	*Order Details.Kitchen*	*Is greater than*	*0*
Or	*Order Details.Wardrobe*	*Is greater than*	*0*
And	*Customers.Town*	*Equals*	*Cullenstown*

Each criterion you add through the *Add Criteria* dialog box is combined with all the other criteria you already entered using the selected logical operator.

By adding the *AND Customers.Town Equals Cullenstown* criterion last, you combined this requirement with *all* of the *Order Details* criteria. You could not have done this if you had added the *Town* criterion first.

When you have finished adding criteria, click **Close**.

8. Select **File | Return Data to Microsoft Excel**, or click the **Return Data** toolbar button.

Return Data button

9. Save your workbook.

Well done! You just created an advanced filter in MS Query, combining a range of criteria using both logical AND and logical OR.

Microsoft Query allows you to select any column in the database when you create a criterion, not only those that you are importing. This makes Microsoft Query a more powerful filtering tool than the *Query Wizard*.

Over to you: mandatory

Next, you will edit the query results on the OUTDOOR worksheet to show similar results.

- On the OUTDOOR worksheet of MFPF_ORD.XLS (or Ex3.5-MFPF_ORD.xls), add an advanced filter to the query results to show records for customers in Cullenstown who ordered at least one item of outdoor furniture.
- Save your workbook.

Chapter summary

A delimited text file is a text file in which columns of information are separated from each other by a particular character or set of characters, known as delimiters. Excel allows you to import data from delimited text files using the *Text Import Wizard*. You can choose to import all of the columns in a delimited text file, or only a subset of them. You can also specify at which row of the text file you should start the import.

Excel also allows you to import database records using a *query*. A query is a set of rules that say what records, or parts of records, to retrieve from the database, and how to display those data.

When you create a query, you can define a *sort order* for the results. You can sort by the values in any number of columns.

You can also include a filter in your query to import only those records that satisfy specific criteria. Excel's *Query Wizard* allows you to set simple filter requirements based on the values in the database columns you are importing. You can edit your query in Microsoft Query to set much more complex filter requirements based on the values in any of the database columns.

Quick Quiz

Circle the answer to each of the following multiple-choice questions about importing data into a spreadsheet.

Q1	A text file in which columns of information are separated from each other by a particular character or set of characters is known as...
A.	Limited.
B.	Unlimited.
C.	Delimited.
D.	Delighted.

Q2	A text qualifier is...
A.	Someone who edits books.
B.	A character used to mark the beginning and end of a data element in a delimited text file.
C.	A character used to indicate whether data are text or numeric.
D.	A character used to indicate that the following text should not be ignored during a data import.

Q3	Any character can be used as a delimiter.
A.	True.
B.	False.

Q4	Simple database queries are created using...
A.	An Excel template.
B.	The Text Import Wizard.
C.	The Query Wizard.
D.	Microsoft Query.

Q5	The Query Wizard allows you to combine criteria for different columns using logical AND or logical OR.
A.	True.
B.	False.

Q6	Microsoft Query allows you to combine criteria for different columns using logical AND or logical OR.
A.	True.
B.	False.

Q7	If the data in the source file changes after you have imported it to Excel, you must delete your imported data and start over to update it.
A.	True.
B.	False.

Answers **1:** C; **2:** B; **3:** A; **4:** C; **5:** B; **6:** A; **7:** B.

Chapter 4: Sorting data in a spreadsheet

In this chapter

In ECDL 3 or ECDL 4, you learned how to sort the information in a column numerically and alphabetically, in ascending and descending order.

When you defined a query in *Chapter 3*, you edited that query to sort the returned data by the values in multiple columns. Now, you will find out how to sort by multiple columns in an Excel spreadsheet.

You will learn how to use Excel's custom sort orders to sort data in a non-alphabetic and non-numeric order, for example, by days of the week.

Finally, you will learn how to define a custom sort order of your own.

New skills

At the end of this chapter you should be able to:

- Sort by the values in multiple columns
- Sort columns using a custom sort order
- Create a custom list

New words

At the end of this chapter you should be able to explain the following terms:

- Custom list

Syllabus reference

The following syllabus items are covered in this chapter:
- AM 4.2.1.1 – Sort data by multiple columns.
- AM 4.2.1.2 – Perform custom sorts.

Sorting data in Excel

Typically, you will sort data in an Excel spreadsheet so that they are presented in a way that is easier to read and understand. For example, you might sort a list of birthdays in chronological order, or a list of mountain ranges by height.

In ECDL 3 or ECDL 4, you used Excel's **Sort** command to sort the data in a single column into ascending or descending order. In fact, you can sort data by the values in up to three columns in Excel.

> **Note:** When you sorted records in a database query, there was no limit to the number of columns you could sort by.

> **Note:** A trick to sort data by the values in four columns is to sort by the least important column first, then to perform a three-column sort on the resulting list.

Sorting multiple columns at the same time

Mrs Murphy liked the way you sorted the results from the query you created earlier. She would like to see the data on the *COMPLETE* worksheet of MFPF_ORD.XLS sorted by customer, with the orders from each customer sorted in reverse chronological order.

In the following exercise you will rearrange the rows on the *COMPLETE* worksheet of MFPF_ORD.XLS as Mrs Murphy asked.

Exercise 4.1: Sorting by multiple columns

1. Open MFPF_ORD.XLS (or Ex3.5-OTYM1-MFPF_ORD.xls) and go to the *COMPLETE* worksheet.
2. Select columns *A* to *J*, then select **Data | Sort...**.
   The *Sort* dialog box opens.

Note: If you select just one row of data in the table of order details – for example, *A1:J1* or *A12:J12* – then click **Data | Sort...**, Excel will open a dialog box asking you if you want it to automatically expand your selection to include adjacent data. If you choose to expand your selection, Excel will perform the sort operation on the cell range *A2:J55*. This is useful where the data you want to sort is not the only information in the relevant columns of your spreadsheet.

3. In the *Sort by* field, select *CompanyName* and *Ascending*.
   In the *Then by* field, select *OrderDate* and *Descending*.

4. Click **OK**.
   Your data are now sorted alphabetically by the values in the *CompanyName* column, with the orders for each company listed in reverse chronological order.

5. Save your workbook when you are done.

Over to you: optional

To impress Mrs Murphy even more, you decide to rearrange the data on the *COMPLETE* worksheet again, this time sorting by three columns!

- Open MFPF_ORD.XLS (or Ex4.1-MFPF_ORD.xls).

- First, you will sort by *Town* in ascending order, then by *CompanyName* in ascending order, and finally by *OrderDate* in descending order.
  All of the orders for each customer will still be grouped together, as Mrs Murphy requested, but now the customers themselves will be grouped according to which town they are from.

Custom sort orders

Look at the following column of data, which lists the first three months of the year in an arbitrary order:

	A	B	C
1	January		
2	March		
3	February		

What order do you think it should be sorted in? If you tried simply to sort the months in ascending order, Excel would sort them alphabetically, resulting in:

	A	B	C
1	February		
2	January		
3	March		

Chances are, you would rather sort the data so that they appear in this order:

	A	B	C
1	January		
2	February		
3	March		

How do you tell Excel that you want to use a special order for sorting columns containing the months of the year? You use a custom sort order.

Using a custom sort order

A custom sort order is defined using a custom list which lists the values in the required order. Excel comes with custom lists for days of the week and months of the year by default.

> **Custom list**
>
> *A custom list is a list which specifies a non-alphabetic and non-numeric order for a series of data elements, for example, the days of the week in chronological order.*

Custom lists are used when performing custom sorts, and can also be used to autofill cell ranges. You learned about AutoFill functionality in ECDL 3 or ECDL 4.

In the next exercise you will use a custom sort order to sort cells containing entries for the months January, February and March into their usual chronological order.

Exercise 4.2: Sorting using a custom sort order

1. Open a new workbook based on the default template.
2. In the cell range *A1:A3*, enter the values *January*, *March*, *February*.
3. Select the cell range, and select **Data | Sort...**.
   The *Sort* dialog box opens.

4. In the *Sort by* field, select *Column A*.
5. Click **Options...**.
   The *Sort Options* dialog box opens.
6. In the *First key sort order* field, select the entry beginning *January, February, March*, then click **OK**.

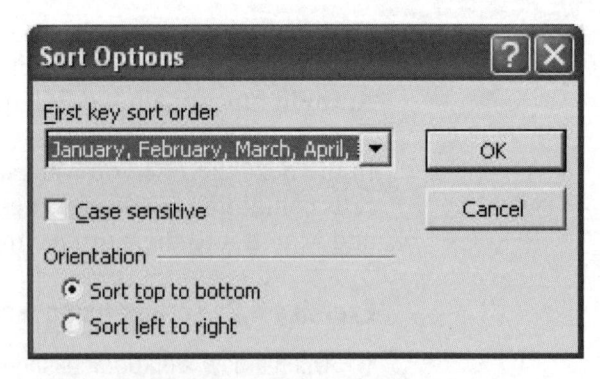

7. Click **OK** again on the *Sort* dialog box.
   The data in the cell range are now sorted in the order you would usually expect.

	A	B	C
1	January		
2	February		
3	March		

8. Close your workbook *without saving* when you are done.

Defining a custom list

You can add any number of additional custom lists to Excel; for example, you can list employee names by seniority, or groceries according to which aisle they are on in the supermarket. Custom lists are stored as part of Excel, and will be available to you in any workbook.

Mr Murphy has heard about your superior sorting skills. He asks you to sort order information by how far away each customer is. This will let him stock the delivery van so that the goods for the furthest away customer are loaded first and unloaded last.

In the next exercise you will create a custom list that lists the customers in order of how far away they are.

Exercise 4.3: Adding a custom list to Excel

1. Start Excel if it is not already started. It does not matter which workbook is open, because your custom list will be stored as part of Excel.
2. Select **Tools | Options...**.

The *Options* dialog box opens.

3. Select the **Custom lists** tab.
   The custom lists already known to Excel are shown in the *Custom lists* area.

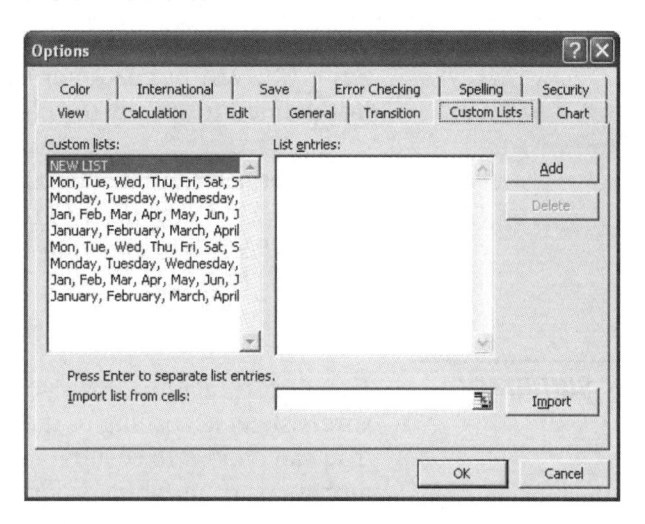

4. In the *Custom lists* area, select *NEW LIST*, then add the following data in the *List entries* area:
   Joe's Hardware
   Cullenstown Garden Centre
   The DIY Centre
   Mullens
   Garden Glories
   Liam Kinsella and Sons
   Pay close attention to the spelling and punctuation used. Later, Excel will use this list to sort entries in your spreadsheet, and it will not recognize values that do not exactly match those in this list.

   Note: To guarantee that you use the correct spelling and punctuation when creating this list, you could copy and paste each company name (in the order given above) from the imported data to an empty cell range, then use the *Import list from cells* field at the bottom of the *Custom Lists* tab to tell Excel to base the entries in your new list on that cell range. If you do this, delete the cell range you use to create the list when you're done.

5. Click **Add**.
   Your new entry is now shown in the *Custom lists* area.
6. Click **OK**.

Well done! You just added a custom list to Excel. You will be able to use this list in future to specify a custom sort order when you sort data, or autofill cell ranges in any spreadsheet.

Over to you: optional

Next, you will sort the data on the *COMPLETE* worksheet in MFPF_ORD.XLS by customer name, using the custom list you just defined to specify the correct sort order.

- Use the custom list of customer names you defined in *Exercise 4.3* on page 43 to sort the entries on the *COMPLETE* worksheet in MFPF_ORD.XLS (or Ex4.1-MFPF_ORD.xls).

Chapter summary

Excel's sort facility allows you to reorder the rows in a spreadsheet according to the values in multiple columns. You can choose to sort data in ascending or descending alphabetic or numeric order, or in a custom order.

Custom sort orders allow you to sort data in a specific non-alphabetic and non-numeric order. Custom sorts use custom lists to define the correct order to use when sorting data.

A custom list is a list that specifies a non-alphabetic and non-numeric order for a series of data elements, for example, the days of the week in chronological order.

You can create your own custom lists in Excel.

Quick Quiz

Circle the answer to each of the following multiple-choice questions about sorting data in spreadsheets.

Q1	Excel allows you to sort data in how many columns at once?
A.	1
B.	2
C.	3
D.	4

Q2	Custom sorts allow you to sort data by:
A.	Days of the week.
B.	Months of the year.
C.	Any other custom list of values.
D.	All of the above.

Q3	To add a custom list to Excel:
A.	You must download it from the Microsoft website.
B.	You can add it through the *Options* dialog box.
C.	You should define a new template with the required data.
D.	You can't add custom lists – you have to make do with the default ones.

Q4	Custom lists are associated with the spreadsheet open at the time you create the lists.
A.	True.
B.	False.

Q5	When sorting using a custom list, Excel ignores whitespace and punctuation differences.
A.	True.
B.	False.

Answers **1:** C; **2:** D; **3:** B; **4:** B; **5:** B.

Chapter 5: Naming cells and adding comments

In this chapter

When dealing with large spreadsheets, it is easy to lose track of what particular cell ranges are for, and why you have decided to perform your calculations in a particular way.

Usually, you use labels to indicate what the contents of a particular cell, row or column represent. Sometimes, because of the layout or complexity of your data, it might not be possible to label them in this way. For example, you may want to assign a single overall label to a group of labelled cells or cell ranges.

In this chapter you will learn about two other ways you can assign additional information to a cell or cell range: custom names and comments. Custom names can be used to identify cells or cell ranges in calculations as well as for pure labelling purposes.

New skills

At the end of this chapter you should be able to:

- Give a cell or cell range a custom name
- Navigate a worksheet or workbook using custom names
- Use a named cell or cell range in a formula
- Add comments to your spreadsheet
- Read comments in a spreadsheet
- Edit spreadsheet comments
- Delete spreadsheet comments

New words

At the end of this chapter you should be able to explain the following terms:

- Custom name
- Comment

Syllabus reference

The following syllabus items are covered in this chapter:
- AM 4.1.1.1 – Name cell range(s) in a worksheet.
- AM 4.4.3.4 – Add or remove worksheet comments.
- AM 4.4.3.5 – Edit worksheet comments.

Cell names

Every cell in a worksheet has a unique name.

By default, a cell's name is determined by the column and row it occupies. For example, *A1* is the default name of the cell that appears in column *A* of row *1* in every Excel worksheet.

When you select a cell, its name appears in the *Name Box* to the left of the formula bar.

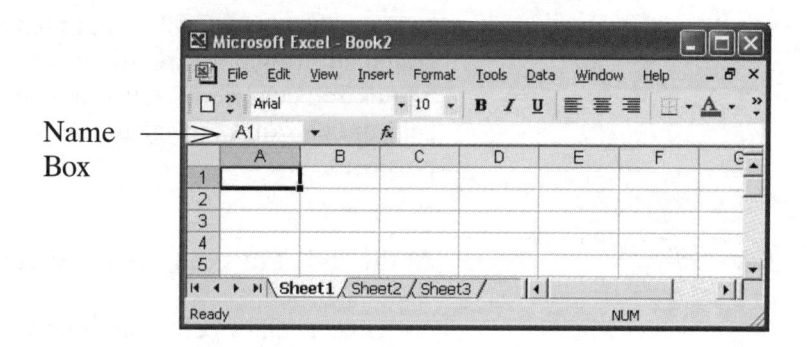

Name Box

You can also enter a cell's name in the *Name Box* and press **ENTER** to select that cell.

Custom cell names

You can associate a custom name with any cell or cell range. Because cell names must be unique, you can only use a particular name once in any workbook. But you can associate as many different custom names as you like with any cell or cell range.

Custom name
A custom name is a unique name in a workbook, which can be used to identify a cell or cell range.

Once you have assigned a name in a workbook, if you try to reassign it by typing it in the *Name Box* a second time, you will instead be moved to the cell or cell range that already has that name. If you want to change which cell or cell range a name is associated with, you can delete the name from the workbook and reassign it, or you can simply edit the cell range associated with the name. To do this, click **Insert | Name | Define...** to open the *Define Name* dialog box, select the mis-assigned name and either click **Delete** or redefine the appropriate cell range in the *Refers to* field.

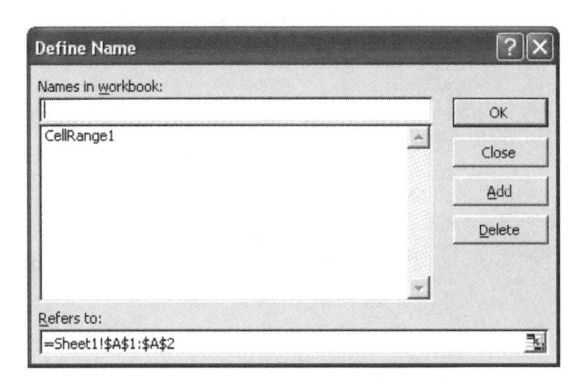

Note: If you *cut* (not copy) and paste a cell, any custom name assigned to the original cell is transferred to the new cell. However, if you cut a cell from the middle of a custom named cell range, the name remains associated with the original cell range – it cannot be split across locations. The custom name for a cell range will only move if *every* cell in the range is cut and pasted to a new location.

You can see a list of all of the custom names associated with cells and cell ranges in your workbook either in the *Define Name* dialog box, or by simply clicking the down arrow to the right of the *Name Box*. If you select a name from the *Name Box* drop-down list, Excel will instantly select the cell or cell range that uses that name.

Custom cell names and formulae	You can use custom cell names instead of the default ones when you refer to cells and cell ranges in formulae. This can often make formulae easier to read and to edit.

Have a look at cell *C15*, which has been named *INC_TOT*, on the *INCOMING* worksheet of MFPF_FINANCE.XLS. It contains the formula:

=*SUM(Products)+SUM(Delivery)*

Compare this to:

=*SUM(B2:B13)+SUM(C2:C13)*

Although each formula calculates the exact same thing, the first is much easier to read and understand.

Assigning a custom name to a cell range

There are a lot of data in the MFPF_FINANCE.XLS workbook. Naming particular cells and cell ranges will make the workbook easier to use.

In the next exercise, you are going to assign a custom name to a cell range.

Exercise 5.1: Naming a cell range

1. Open MFPF_FINANCE.XLS (or Ex3.1-OTYM1-MFPF_FINANCE.xls) and go to the *SALES TOTALS* worksheet.
2. Select the cell range *A1:H13*.
   This cell range will be used to hold the monthly sales figures for each product.
3. In the *Name Box*, enter the word *SALES* and press **Enter**.

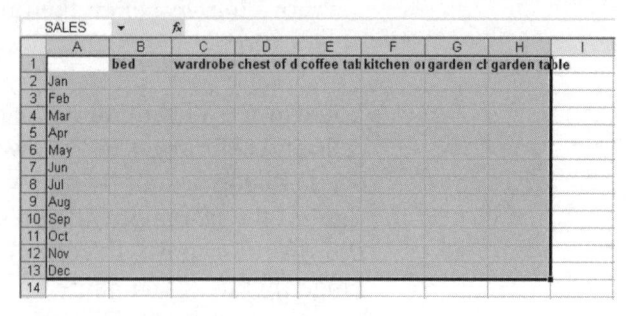

4. Save the workbook.

If you look at the *Name Box* list, *SALES* is now included.

The procedure for naming a single cell is exactly the same.

Over to you: mandatory

Next, you will name some cell ranges yourself, and then use the custom names in a formula.

- On the *OUTGOING* worksheet of MFPF_FINANCE.XLS (or Ex5.1-MFPF_FINANCE.xls), name the cell ranges referring to particular payment types (for example, assign the name *RENT* to the cell range *B2:B13*).
- Enter a formula in cell *C15* which adds up the totals for each payment type for the year, using the cell range names you just defined.
- Assign the name *TOTAL_OUTGOING* to cell *C15*; then save your workbook.

Comments

Comments are a useful way to add notes to cells in your worksheets. You might add a comment to remind yourself of why you calculated a value using one method rather than another. Or you might use a comment to let a colleague who will work with the spreadsheet later know what needs to be done next.

Comment
A comment is a type of note that can be associated with a spreadsheet cell.

Comment text is normally hidden from view, so that you can continue working with an uncluttered spreadsheet. A cell with an associated comment has a small red triangle in its top-right corner:

	A	B
1	This cell has a comment	
2		

The *Reviewing* toolbar contains buttons for most of the commands you will use when creating, reading, editing and deleting comments. If you cannot see the *Reviewing* toolbar, you can open it by selecting **View | Toolbars | Reviewing**.

Adding comments

Earlier, you assigned the name *SALES* to a cell range in MFPF_FINANCE.XLS. At the moment there are no numeric data in this cell range. What is the cell range there for? How will someone else editing the worksheet know if it will be required later, or if you have already used it and it can be deleted?

In the next exercise, you will add a comment to the *SALES* cell range explaining what it represents and what it will be used for.

Exercise 5.2: Adding a comment to a cell

1. Go to the cell range named *SALES* in MFPF_FINANCE.XLS (or Ex5.1-OTYM1-MFPF_FINANCE.xls).
2. Right-click cell *A1*, and select **Insert Comment** from the shortcut menu that appears.
   – or –
   Select cell *A1* and click the **New Comment** button on the *Reviewing* toolbar.
   A comment box opens.

New Comment button

3. Enter the following text in the comment box:
   This table shows the total sales of each product type each month. The data will be used later to calculate our incoming sales revenue on the INCOMING worksheet.
4. If you cannot see all of the comment text, resize the comment box by clicking and dragging one of the white resize handles that appear around the edge of the box.
5. Save your workbook when you are done.

Reading comments

There are several different ways to display the comment associated with a cell in order to read it:

- If you place your cursor over the cell with the comment, a pop-up box displays the contents of the comment. The pop-up box closes when you move your cursor away.

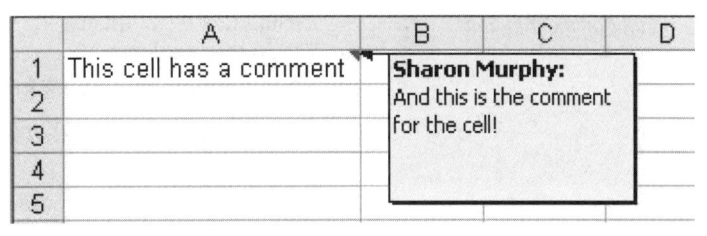

	A	B	C	D
1	This cell has a comment	**Sharon Murphy:**		
2		And this is the comment		
3		for the cell!		
4				
5				

Show/Hide Comment button

- If you select the cell with the comment, you can click the **Show/Hide Comment** button on the *Reviewing* toolbar to display the comment associated with that cell. The comment will remain open until you click the **Show/Hide Comment** button a second time.
- If you right-click a cell with an associated comment, you can select **Show Comment** from the shortcut menu that opens. The comment will remain open until you right-click the cell again and select **Hide Comment** from the shortcut menu.

You can also choose to display all spreadsheet comments. There are two ways to do this:

- If you select **View | Comments**, all comments will be displayed. You can deselect **View | Comments** to hide all comments again.

Show/Hide All Comments button

- If you click the **Show/Hide All Comments** button on the *Reviewing* toolbar, all comments will be displayed. Click the **Show/Hide All Comments** button again to hide the comments.

Editing comments

You can reopen a comment to edit its text at any time.

In the next exercise you will edit the comment you added to the *SALES* cell range in *Exercise 5.2* on page 52.

Exercise 5.3: Editing a comment

1. Go to the cell range named *SALES* in MFPF_FINANCE.XLS (or Ex5.2-MFPF_FINANCE.xls).
2. Right-click cell *A1*, and select **Edit Comment** from the shortcut menu that appears.
   – or –

Edit Comment button

Select cell *A1* and click the **Edit Comment** button on the *Reviewing* toolbar.
The comment box opens for editing.

3. Go to the end of the text you entered earlier and add the following text:
and also our materials expenses on the OUTGOING worksheet.

4. Save your workbook when you are done.

Deleting comments

If you select a cell with an associated comment and press **DELETE**, you delete the cell contents – but not the comment! This means that you can add a comment saying what the value in the cell represents, and not worry about losing your comment if you delete or change the value in the cell.

In the next exercise you will find out how to delete the comment you added to the *SALES* cell range in *Exercise 5.2* on page 52.

Exercise 5.4: Removing a comment

1. Go to the cell range named *SALES* in MFPF_FINANCE.XLS (or Ex5.3-MFPF_FINANCE.xls).

2. Right-click cell *A1*, and select **Delete Comment** from the shortcut menu that appears.
   – or –

Delete Comment button

Select cell *A1* and click the **Delete Comment** button on the *Reviewing* toolbar.
The comment is deleted from the cell.

3. Save and close your workbook when you are done.

Chapter summary

Every cell in every Excel worksheet has a default name which is defined by the column and row it is in, for example, *A1*. You can assign a unique custom name to a cell or cell range. These custom names can be used in formulae.

A comment is a type of note that can be associated with a spreadsheet cell. A small red triangle in a cell indicates that it has an associated comment. Usually comments are hidden so that you can work with an uncluttered worksheet.

Quick Quiz

Circle the answer to each of the following multiple-choice questions about naming cells and adding comments.

Q1	Once you name a cell, there is no way to unname it.
A.	True.
B.	False.

Q2	Comments are always open and visible once you add them to a workbook.
A.	True.
B.	False.

Q3	You can only assign a particular name to one cell or cell range in a given workbook.
A.	True.
B.	False.

Q4	If you enter a name that's already been used in the current workbook in the Name box...
A.	Excel reassigns the name to the currently selected cell/cell range.
B.	A warning dialog box appears.
C.	Excel replaces the data in the selected cell/cell range with the data from the cell/cell range already using that name.
D.	Excel selects the cell range already using that name instead.

Q5	The toolbar that allows you to view, add, edit and delete comments is called...
A.	The *Comments* toolbar.
B.	The *Reviewing* toolbar.
C.	The *Notes* toolbar.
D.	The *Editing* toolbar.

Q6	Cell and cell range names can be used in formulas in Excel.
A.	True.
B.	False.

Answers   **1:** B; **2:** B; **3:** A; **4:** D; **5:** B; **6:** A.

Chapter 6: Using Paste Special

In this chapter

Every cell in an Excel spreadsheet has many different types of information associated with it. It will have some kind of formatting. It may contain a value or formula or an associated comment.

Usually, when you copy a cell's contents and paste them somewhere else, you paste *all* of the information associated with that cell.

Excel's **Paste Special** command allows you to select specific elements of a copied cell's information to paste. You can also manipulate copied data in a variety of ways before pasting them to their destination cell(s).

New skills

At the end of this chapter you should be able to:

- Paste specific elements of copied data to a destination cell
- Perform simple mathematical operations using **Paste Special**
- Create links between cells using **Paste Special**

New words

There are no new words in this chapter.

Syllabus reference

The following syllabus items are covered in this chapter:
- AM 4.1.1.5 – Use paste special options.

Why Paste Special?

When you copy a data element from one cell in an Excel spreadsheet, and paste it to another cell, Excel pastes *all* of the information associated with the cell you copied to the new cell.

If you copied the value 12, formatted in 14pt Arial with a bright yellow background, then when you paste the value to a new cell, it will be formatted in 14pt Arial with a bright yellow background! If the cell you copied contained a formula, you probably will not even see the same value when you paste it, unless the formula used absolute cell references (for example, *$A$1*).

When you use the **Paste Special** command instead of **Paste**, the *Paste Special* dialog box opens, and you can choose which part or parts of the data you really want to paste.

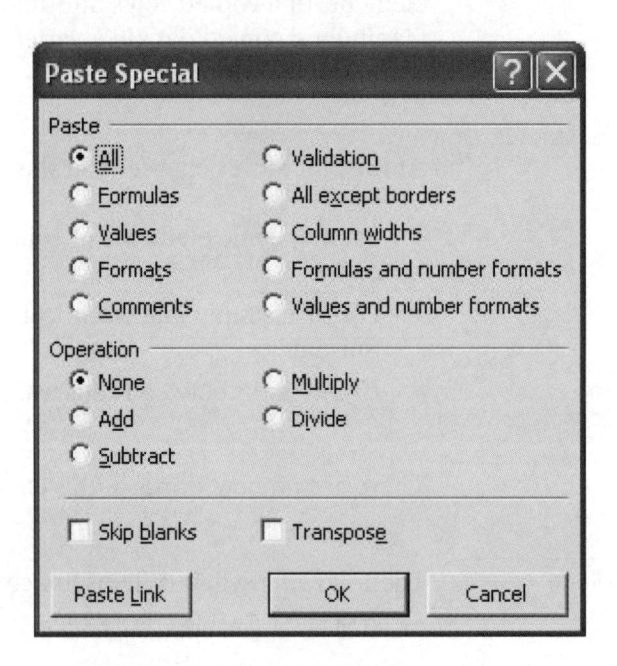

Note: The Paste Special dialog box shown above only appears if you are pasting Excel spreadsheet cells. If you are posting any other kind of data, for example text or images, you will see the standard Microsoft Office *Paste Special* dialog box.

Pasting different types of information

In the *Paste* area of Excel's *Paste Special* dialog box, you can choose which part, or parts, of the copied data you want to paste to the destination cell(s).

You can only choose one option at a time from the *Paste* area. If you want to paste a combination of the different information types associated with the data – for example, a formula and its associated comment – you must use **Paste Special** more than once to paste each piece of information.

The following table lists the different options in the *Paste* area of the *Paste Special* dialog box and explains what each one does.

Option	Action
All	Paste all types of information associated with the data in the copied cell(s).
Formulas	Paste the formula information from the copied cell(s) only. If there is no formula associated with a copied cell, the value in the cell is pasted instead.
Values	Paste the value information from the copied cell(s). If a copied cell contains a formula, the result of that formula is pasted as a value instead.
Formats	Paste the formatting information from the copied cell.
All except borders	Paste the formula or value, and the formatting data from the copied cell, but don't include border formatting.
Column widths	Paste the column width from the copied cell.
Comments	Paste the comment from the copied cell.
Validation	Paste the validation, or data entry, rules from the copied cell.

In the following exercises, you will copy cells from the workbook PASTE_SPECIAL.XLS, and use the options in the

Paste Special dialog box to paste particular types of information associated with the copied data to destination cells.

Note: To deselect a cell range after you have copied it, press **ESC**.

Note: Remember that when you paste a cell range, the destination cell range must be the same size as the original cell range – you can't paste 5 cells worth of data into just one cell, and Excel won't automatically add extra cells for you! If your selected destination is the wrong shape/size, Excel takes the top left cell you have selected as the starting point for pasting data and pastes to a range of the appropriate dimension starting from that cell. If this will result in Excel overwriting existing data, a warning message appears, so you can cancel the paste and reselect an area to paste to.

Exercise 6.1: Pasting formulae

1. Open the PASTE_SPECIAL.XLS workbook.

	A	B	C	D	E	F	G	H
1								
2		2	3	4	5	6	10	
3		4	6	8	10	0	10	
4		6	9	12	15	18	10	
5		8	12	16	20	0	10	
6		10	15	20	25	30	10	
7		12	18	24	30		10	
8		14	21	28	35	42	10	
9		16	24	32	40		10	
10		18	27	36	45	54	10	
11		20	30	40	50		10	
12	yOuR vAlUe HeRe:							
13	TOTALS	110						
14								

2. Copy the contents of cell *B13*.
3. Select the cell range *C13:E13*.
4. Select **Edit | Paste Special...**.
5. In the *Paste* area select *Formulas* and click **OK**.
   The relative SUM formula from cell *B13* is the only information pasted to the cells in the cell range *C13:E13*.

Exercise 6.2: Pasting values

1. Copy the contents of cell *B13*.

2. Select cell *J2*.
3. Select **Edit | Paste Special...**.
4. In the *Paste* area select *Values* and click **OK**.
   The result of the formula in cell *B13* is pasted to cell *J2*.

Exercise 6.3: Pasting formats

1. Copy the contents of cell *A13*.
2. Select the cell range *C13:E13*.
3. Select **Edit | Paste Special...**.
4. In the *Paste* area select *Formats* and click **OK**.
   The cell and font formatting from cell *A13* is pasted to cells *C13:E13*.

Exercise 6.4: Pasting all cell information except borders

1. Copy the cell range named *Table1*.
2. Select cell *B15*.
3. Select **Edit | Paste Special...**.
4. In the *Paste* area, select *All except borders* and click **OK**.
   All of the copied cell information except borders are pasted to a cell range starting in cell *B15*.

Exercise 6.5: Pasting column widths

1. Copy the cell range named *Table1*.
2. Select cell *H15*.
3. Select **Edit | Paste Special...**.
4. In the *Paste* area select *Column widths* and click **OK**.
   The column widths used in *Table1* are pasted to a cell range starting in cell *H15*.

Exercise 6.6: Pasting comments

1. Copy the contents of cell *B13*.
2. Select the cell range *C13:E13*.
3. Select **Edit | Paste Special...**.
4. In the *Paste* area select *Comments* and click **OK**.
   The comment in cell *B13* is pasted to cells *C13:E13*.

Exercise 6.7: Pasting validation

1. Copy the contents of cell *B12*.
   Cell *B12* has associated validation rules that allow you to enter only whole numbers in the cell.
2. Select the cell range *C12:E12*.
3. Select **Edit | Paste Special...**.
4. In the *Paste* area select *Validation* and click **OK**.
   The validation rules from cell *B12* are pasted to cells *C12:E12*.

The Operations area

You can combine numeric data from a copied cell with numeric data in a destination cell when you use **Paste Special**. The value in the destination cell is replaced by the result of the operation. Available operations are listed in the *Operation* area of the *Paste Special* dialog box.

The selection you make in the *Operation* area is combined with your selection from the *Paste* area.

The following table lists the different options in the *Operation* area of the *Paste Special* dialog box and explains what each one does:

Option	Action
None	Do not perform any operation.
Add	Add the data in the copied cell(s) to the data in the destination cell(s), and place the result in the destination cell(s).
Subtract	Subtract the data in the copied cell(s) from the data in the destination cell(s), and place the result in the destination cell(s).
Multiply	Multiple the data in the copied cell(s) by the data in the destination cell(s), and place the result in the destination cell(s).
Divide	Divide the data in the destination cell(s) by the data in the copied cell(s), and place the result in the destination cell(s).

In the next exercise, you will use the *Add* operation in the *Paste Special* dialog box to combine numeric data in two cell ranges.

Exercise 6.8: Pasting with operations

1. Copy the contents of cells *B2:B11*.
2. Select the cell range *G2:G11*.
3. Select **Edit | Paste Special...**.
4. In the *Paste* area select *All*.
   In the *Operations* area, select *Add*.
5. Click **OK**.
   The values, formatting, etc. from the cells in the copied range are added to the values in the corresponding cells in the destination cell range, and the totals replace the original values in the cell range *G2:G11*.

Special options

There are three additional special options in the *Paste Special* dialog box: *Skip blanks*, *Transpose* and **Paste Link**.

Skip blanks

A 'blank' cell is one that contains no values or formulae, though it may have any of the other information types associated with it, such as formatting, comments or validation rules.

The *Skip blanks* option can be used in conjunction with options from the *Paste* and *Operations* areas of the *Paste Special* dialog box. If *Skip blanks* is selected, then no information is pasted for any copied cell which does not contain either a value or a formula.

If you try to divide a number by zero in Excel, an error message, *#DIV/0!*, appears in the cell where the calculation was attempted. When you use operations, blank cells are treated as though they contain zeros *unless* you use the *Skip blanks* option. This makes the *Skip blanks* option especially useful when used in combination with the *Divide* operation.

In the next exercise you will use the *Skip blanks* option on the *Paste Special* dialog box to tell Excel to ignore blank cells in a copied cell range when performing a *Divide* operation.

Exercise 6.9: Skip blanks

1. Copy the contents of cells *F2:F11*.
2. Select the cell range *G2:G11*.
3. Select **Edit | Paste Special...**.
4. In the *Paste* area select *Values*.
   In the *Operations* area, select *Divide*.
   Check the box beside *Skip Blanks*.
   Click **OK**.

	A	B	C	D	E	F	G	H
1								
2		2	3	4	5	6	2	
3		4	6	8	10	0	#DIV/0!	
4		6	9	12	15	18	0.888889	
5		8	12	16	20	0	#DIV/0!	
6		10	15	20	25	30	0.666667	
7		12	18	24	30		22	
8		14	21	28	35	42	0.571429	
9		16	24	32	40		26	
10		18	27	36	45	54	0.518519	
11		20	30	40	50		30	
12	yOuR vAlUe HeRe:							
13	TOTALS	110	165	220	275			
14								

In the cell range *G2:G11*, *#DIV/0!* errors are shown in the cells where you actually divided by zero (because that was the value in the copied cell).

But, where the cell in the copied cell range was blank, the value in the pasted range does not change.

Transpose

You can combine the *Transpose* option with selections from the *Paste* and *Operation* areas of the *Paste Special* dialog box. If you copy a range of cells which are in a column orientation, you can use the *Transpose* option to paste them in a row orientation, and vice versa.

In the next exercise you will copy a cell range in a column orientation, and use the *Transpose* option to paste it to another cell range in a row orientation.

Exercise 6.10: Transpose

1. Copy the contents of cells *G2:G11*.
2. Select the cell *A1*.
3. Select **Edit | Paste Special...**.
4. In the *Paste* area select *Values*.

Check the box beside *Transpose*.
Click **OK**.

5. The data from the column of cells *G2:G11* is pasted to the row of cells *A1:A10*.

Paste Link

If it is important that a cell in your spreadsheet should always contain the value from another cell, you can create a link from the second cell to the first.

You can use the **Paste Link** option in the *Paste Special* dialog box to link the destination cell to the copied cell.

If the value in the source cell changes, the value in the destination cell automatically updates to reflect the change.

In fact, a link between cells is even maintained if the source *or* destination cell is moved around in your spreadsheet! A cell's position is changed if you add rows/cells above it, or columns/cells to the left of it, or if you cut (not copy) the cell and paste it somewhere else.

In the next exercise you will create links from cells in a destination range to cells in a source range using the **Paste Link** option.

Exercise 6.11: Paste link

1. Copy the contents of cells *A13.E13*.
2. Select the cell *H13*.
3. Select **Edit | Paste Special....**
4. Click **Paste Link**.
   A link is created from each of the cells in the range *H13:L13* to their corresponding cells in the source range, *A13:E13*.
5. Edit some of the values in cells *A13:E13* and see that the values in cells *H13:L13* update automatically to reflect your changes.
6. Try adding rows/cells above and to the left of some of the cells in *A13:E13* (using options from the **Insert** menu), or *cutting* and pasting cells from that range to somewhere else in your workbook (even another worksheet) – notice that even though the original cells change their positions, the destination cells remain linked to them!

Over to you: optional

Continue to experiment with different combinations of options in the *Paste Special* dialog box, until you are comfortable with it. Save and close PASTE_SPECIAL.XLS when you are done.

Chapter summary

A cell in an Excel spreadsheet has many different types of information associated with it: values, formatting, comments, etc. When you use **Copy** and **Paste** to copy the contents of one cell to another in a worksheet, all of the different information types are pasted. You can use **Paste Special** to select a subset of the information types to paste.

Paste Special allows you to combine numeric data from copied cells with numeric data in destination cells using simple mathematical operations. The results of the operation replace the original values in the destination cells.

The *Skip Blanks* option allows you to choose not to paste any information from blank copied cells. A blank cell is one that contains no value or formula, though it may contain other information, such as formatting or a comment.

The *Transpose* option allows you to change the orientation of the copied cells when you paste them, from row to column, or column to row.

The **Paste Link** option allows you to create a link from a destination cell to a source cell. The value in the destination cell will update automatically if the value or formula in the source cell changes, or even if the location of the source or destination cell changes.

Quick Quiz

Circle the answer to each of the following multiple-choice questions about using **Paste Special** in Excel.

Q1	If you copy a cell range and paste it to a single cell, Excel will automatically add extra cells to contain the data.
A.	True.
B.	False.

Q2	The Skip Blanks option in Paste Special ignores what types of cells? (Circle all that apply.)
A.	Cells with no formatting.
B.	Cells with no numeric data only.
C.	Cells with no numeric *or* text data.
D.	Cells with no formulae.

Q3	Paste Special allows you to combine numeric data from copied cells with numeric data in destination cells using which of the following operations? (Circle all that apply.)
A.	Multiplication.
B.	Average.
C.	Division.
D.	Addition.

Q4	The Transpose option allows you to...
A.	Paste columns of information as rows.
B.	Add a fixed value to every number in the copied range before pasting.
C.	Paste data to the right of the selected cell(s).
D.	Swap the data in the destination cell(s) with the data in the source cell(s).

Q5	If you created a link between two cells, then cut and paste the original cell to a different location, the link...
A.	Points to the same cell and whatever it now contains.
B.	Is updated to the new location of the source cell.
C.	Is deleted.
D.	Changes to an absolute value instead of a link.

Answers

1: B; **2:** C, D; **3:** A, C, D; **4:** A; **5:** B.

Chapter 7: Summarizing data using PivotTables

In this chapter

Occasionally, you will want to create a report summarizing the data in a spreadsheet. Your report will probably perform a particular type of calculation using the data, for example to work out totals or averages of recorded values. You might even want to filter the data you include in a particular calculation to include some information and disregard the rest.

Where the spreadsheets you are working with are large and detailed, creating a summary report can be a complicated and demanding task.

Excel's PivotTable functionality allows you to create dynamic, interactive summaries of data sets.

In this chapter, you will learn how to create and use PivotTables.

New skills

At the end of this chapter you should be able to:

- Create a PivotTable
- Filter data in a PivotTable
- Group data in a PivotTable
- Refresh a PivotTable

New words

At the end of this chapter you should be able to explain the following terms:

- PivotTable
- Field
- Group

Syllabus reference

The following syllabus items are covered in this chapter:

- AM 4.4.1.1 – Create a Pivot Table or a Dynamic Crosstab using defined field names.
- AM 4.4.1.2 – Modify the data source and refresh the Pivot Table or Dynamic Crosstab.
- AM 4.4.1.3 – Group / Display data in a Pivot Table or a Dynamic Crosstab by a defined criterion.

What are PivotTables?

A PivotTable is a useful and powerful Excel tool for summarizing large amounts of information in a dynamic report.

> **PivotTable**
> *A PivotTable is an interactive table which allows you to dynamically create reports summarizing large amounts of data.*

PivotTables can be used to generate reports on data from external databases or from Excel spreadsheets. You do not need to include all of the columns from your data source in a PivotTable, only the ones that are of interest to you.

The columns in your original data are referred to as fields when you include them in a PivotTable. This is to avoid confusion with the columns of the PivotTable itself.

> **Field**
> *A field in a PivotTable corresponds to a column in the data source that the PivotTable is being used to summarize.*

You can select which field or fields on which summary calculations should be performed. Summary functions include sum, average, minimum and maximum.

Example of a PivotTable

Because PivotTables are unusual and may be difficult to understand if you've never seen one before, here's a simple example to look at first, before reading a more detailed description of how PivotTables are laid out and filtered.

This PivotTable is based on the data in the *COMPLETE* worksheet of MFPF_ORD.XLS:

	A	B	C	D
1	Town	Cullenstown ▼		
2				
3	CompanyName ▼	Data ▼	Total	
4	Cullenstown Gard	Sum of Chair	108	
5		Average of Chair2	15.42857143	
6	Joe's Hardware	Sum of Chair	0	
7		Average of Chair2	0	
8	The DIY Centre	Sum of Chair	36	
9		Average of Chair2	3	
10	Total Sum of Chair		144	
11	Total Average of Chair2		4.8	
12				

It calculates:

- The total number of chairs ordered by each company over the year
- The average number of chairs ordered by each company per order

The *Page* has been filtered to show records for a specific *Town* (Cullenstown), and each *Row* of the table applies to a particular *CompanyName*.

The *Data* area includes two different calculations on the data in the *Chair* field: one to calculate the sum, and one to calculate the average. Because two different calculations have been performed on the data from the same field, Excel relabelled the field for each calculation to include a number: *Chair* and *Chair2*.

At the bottom of the PivotTable, grand totals show the total number of chairs ordered by *all* of the companies shown, and the average number of chairs per order overall.

So, now that you've seen what a PivotTable looks like, let's find out a bit more about how it's constructed.

PivotTable layout

When you define the layout for a PivotTable, you add fields to four areas: *Page*, *Row*, *Column* and *Data*.

```
| PAGE |   COLUMN   |
|      |            |
|  ROW |    DATA    |
```

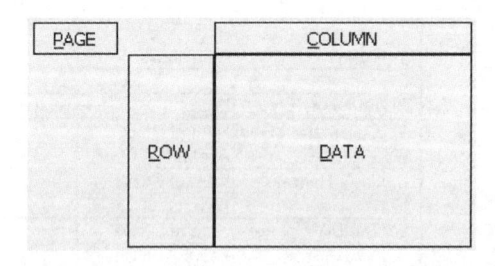

The *Page*, *Column* and *Row* areas show the fields you add and their different values. These values act as labels for the summary results, which are calculated in the *Data* area.

In the earlier example, only the *Page*, *Column* and *Data* areas were used.

You can use the fields in the *Row*, *Column* and *Page* areas to filter the records from the data source which are included in the PivotTable.

Each field in the *Data* area must have a data function associated with it, for example summing the data in the field, averaging the data, or finding a minimum or maximum. The function selected determines what type of summary result is shown for that field. You can calculate more than one type of summary value for the data in a particular field if you want – for example, both the minimum *and* maximum values of a particular data type. As you saw in the earlier example, Excel adds a number to the field label when it is used in more than one calculation.

You do not have to add fields to the *Page*, *Row* and *Column* areas, but the *Data* area *must* contain at least one data function associated with a field in the original data.

Filtering using fields

If you click the arrow to the right of any field name in the *Column/Row* areas of a PivotTable, this opens a drop-down list which contains a list of all the possible values that field might have. The list of values is determined by the values in records in your data source.

You can check or uncheck the box beside each value to include or exclude records where the field has that value.

The *Show All* option allows you to include all possible values for the field.

When you have finished making your selections, click **OK** to return to the PivotTable which will now only display records matching those values.

The drop-down list for a *Page* field is slightly different: it does not have checkboxes beside each value. You can only select one value at a time, but again there is an *All* option which allows you to include all possible values for the field.

Creating PivotTables

You need to produce figures that show MFPF's total sales for each product by month to add to the *SALES TOTALS* worksheet of MFPF_FINANCE.XLS.

In the next exercise, you will begin to calculate these totals by creating a PivotTable to summarize the sales data in the cell range *A1:J55* on the *COMPLETE* worksheet of MFPF_ORD.XLS.

Exercise 7.1: Creating a PivotTable

1. Open MFPF_ORD.XLS (or Ex4.1-MFPF_ORD.xls).
2. Select **Data | PivotTable and PivotChart Report...**.
   – or –
   Click the **PivotTable Wizard** button on the **PivotTable** menu of the *PivotTable* toolbar.
   If you cannot see the *PivotTable* toolbar, you can open it by selecting **View | Toolbars | PivotTable**.
   The *PivotTable and PivotChart Wizard* opens.

PivotTable Wizard button

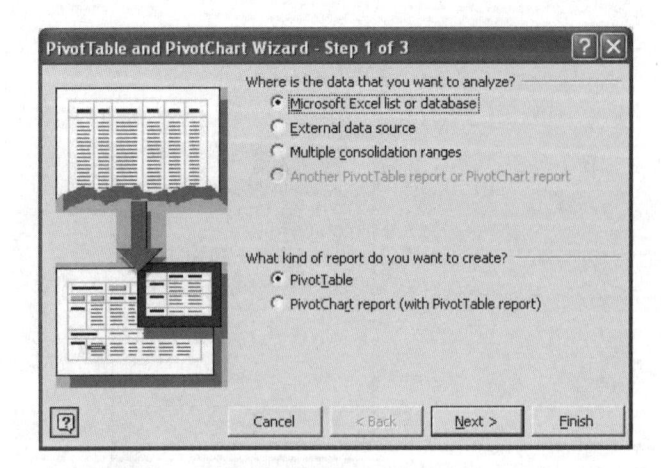

3. In the *Where is the data that you want to analyze?* area, select *Microsoft Excel list or database*.
   In the *What kind of report do you want to create?* area, select *PivotTable*.
   Click **Next**.
   A dialog box opens where you can specify the cell range that contains the source data for the PivotTable.

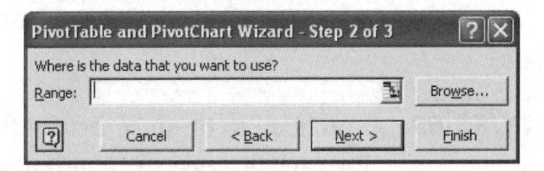

4. Open the *COMPLETE* worksheet and select the cell range *A1:J55*. The reference for the cell range is automatically filled in to the *Range* field.
   Click **Next**.
   A dialog box opens where you can select where to put your PivotTable.

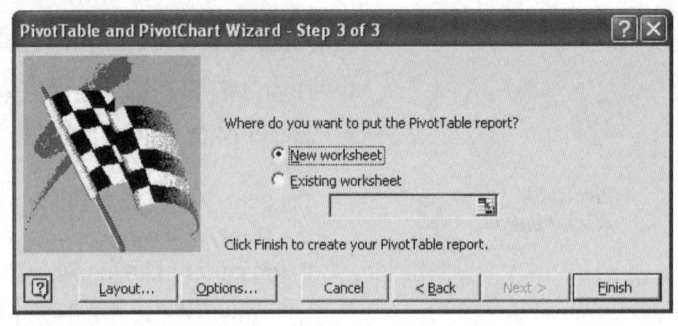

5. Specify that you want to put the PivotTable on a *New worksheet*.

6. Click **Layout**.
   The *PivotTable and PivotChart Wizard – Layout* dialog box opens.

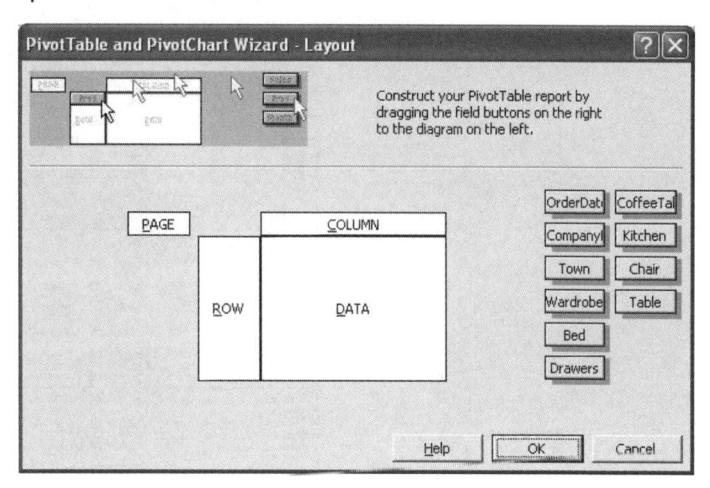

7. You add fields to different areas of the PivotTable by dragging the buttons from the right-hand side of the dialog box to the PivotTable diagram on the left.
   - Drag **OrderDate** to the *Row* area.
   - Drag the following (in order) to the *Data* area: **Bed, Wardrobe, Drawers, CoffeeTable, Kitchen, Chair, Table**.

   The fields in the *Data* area are labelled to indicate the data function associated with them.

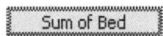

   For this exercise, they should all use the data function *Sum of*. You can change the data function for a field by double-clicking the field and selecting a function from the list that appears.

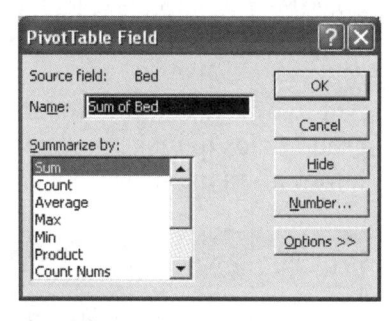

   Click **OK**.
8. Click **Finish**.

ECDL Advanced Spreadsheets for Microsoft® Office XP and 2003

The PivotTable is added to your workbook on a new worksheet. It is laid out according to the settings you made.

	A	B	C	D
1		Drop Page Fields Here		
2				
3	OrderDate ▼	Data ▼	Total	
4	03/01/2000 00:00	Sum of Bed	6	
5		Sum of Wardrobe	0	
6		Sum of Drawers	12	
7		Sum of CoffeeTable	2	
8		Sum of Kitchen	0	
9		Sum of Chair	0	
10		Sum of Table	0	
11	05/01/2000 00:00	Sum of Bed	4	
12		Sum of Wardrobe	6	
13		Sum of Drawers	8	
14		Sum of CoffeeTable	8	
15		Sum of Kitchen	10	
16		Sum of Chair	0	
17		Sum of Table	0	
18	24/01/2000 00:00	Sum of Bed	0	
19		Sum of Wardrobe	0	
20		Sum of Drawers	8	
21		Sum of CoffeeTable	6	
22		Sum of Kitchen	10	
23		Sum of Chair	0	
24		Sum of Table	0	
25	03/02/2000 00:00	Sum of Bed	0	
26		Sum of Wardrobe	2	
27		Sum of Drawers	2	

9. Name the new worksheet *PIVOT* and save your workbook.

Grouping data in PivotTables

You now have 360 rows of data showing sales totals for each furniture type on particular dates. You also have a grand total for sales of each furniture type for the year. You want to know the total for each month.

You could select a subset of *OrderDates* for each month and take the grand totals calculated for those, but that would take a lot of time and clicking.

Not to worry! Another feature of PivotTables is that you can group fields to make it easier to view or select subsets of information in one go.

> **Group**
>
> *A group is a set of objects that is treated as a single object.*

There are two ways to group data in a PivotTable: manually or automatically.

If you group data manually, you select all of the cells you want to group together, then join them together in a group.

If you group data automatically, you select a single cell in the appropriate field, then let Excel automatically determine possible ways the data can be grouped and confirm which way you want the grouping to be carried out. For example, if you selected a cell in a date field, Excel might suggest grouping the dates by time, day, month, quarter or year:

If the field contains numbers, Excel might suggest grouping in 2s, 5s, 10s, etc.:

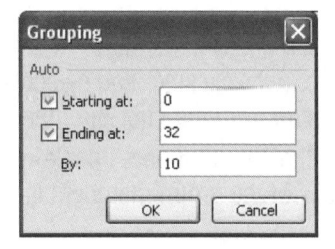

On occasion, Excel may be unable to suggest a way of grouping the data in a field, in which case, you'll need to be able to carry out a manual grouping. For this reason, in the next exercise, you will create a group for all of the order dates in January manually to see how it works.

Exercise 7.2: Grouping data in a PivotTable

1. Go to the *PIVOT* worksheet of MFPF_ORD.XLS (or Ex7.1-MFPF_ORD.xls).

2. In the *OrderDate* field, select all or part of *each* cell that contains a January date.
3. Right-click and select **Group and Show Detail | Group** from the shortcut menu which appears.
   An extra field (*OrderDate2*) is added to the *Column* area of the PivotTable.
   An entry in this column called *Group1* covers all the cells in *OrderDate* related to January.

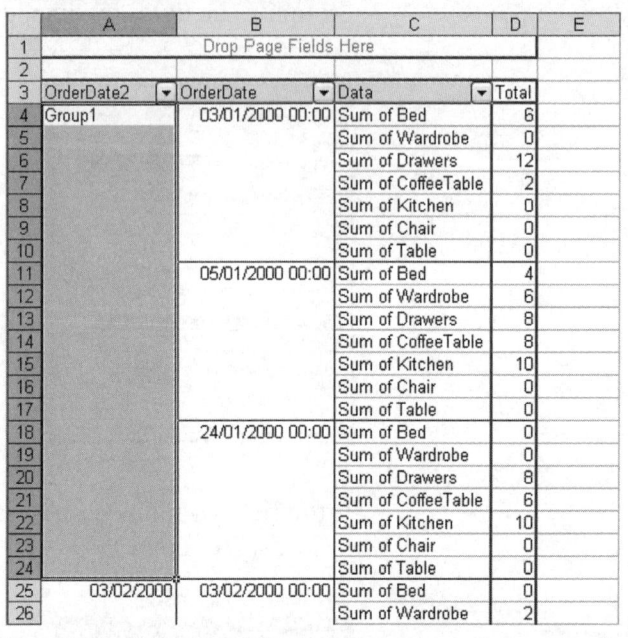

	A	B	C	D	E
1		Drop Page Fields Here			
2					
3	OrderDate2	OrderDate	Data	Total	
4	Group1	03/01/2000 00:00	Sum of Bed	6	
5			Sum of Wardrobe	0	
6			Sum of Drawers	12	
7			Sum of CoffeeTable	2	
8			Sum of Kitchen	0	
9			Sum of Chair	0	
10			Sum of Table	0	
11		05/01/2000 00:00	Sum of Bed	4	
12			Sum of Wardrobe	6	
13			Sum of Drawers	8	
14			Sum of CoffeeTable	8	
15			Sum of Kitchen	10	
16			Sum of Chair	0	
17			Sum of Table	0	
18		24/01/2000 00:00	Sum of Bed	0	
19			Sum of Wardrobe	0	
20			Sum of Drawers	8	
21			Sum of CoffeeTable	6	
22			Sum of Kitchen	10	
23			Sum of Chair	0	
24			Sum of Table	0	
25	03/02/2000	03/02/2000 00:00	Sum of Bed	0	
26			Sum of Wardrobe	2	

You can ungroup the dates in any group again by selecting the group, right-clicking, and selecting **Group and Show Detail | Ungroup** from the shortcut menu which appears.

4. With the data grouped, double-click the group name to hide the details of the group members in the *OrderDate* field.

	A	B	C	D	E
1		Drop Page Fields Here			
2					
3	OrderDate2	OrderDate	Data	Total	
4	Group1		Sum of Bed	10	
5			Sum of Wardrobe	6	
6			Sum of Drawers	28	
7			Sum of CoffeeTable	16	
8			Sum of Kitchen	20	
9			Sum of Chair	0	
10			Sum of Table	0	
11	03/02/2000	03/02/2000 00:00	Sum of Bed	0	
12			Sum of Wardrobe	2	

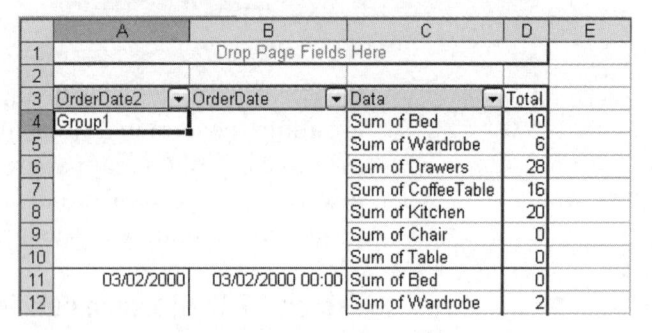

Now the numbers shown in the *Data* area refer to the month as a whole instead of to each day in that group.

5. To rename the group to something more meaningful, select the text *Group1*, and in the formula bar enter the text *January* and press **ENTER**.
   The group is renamed.

	A	B	C	D	E
1		Drop Page Fields Here			
2					
3	OrderDate2	OrderDate	Data	Total	
4	January		Sum of Bed	10	
5			Sum of Wardrobe	6	
6			Sum of Drawers	28	
7			Sum of CoffeeTable	16	
8			Sum of Kitchen	20	
9			Sum of Chair	0	
10			Sum of Table	0	
11	03/02/2000	03/02/2000 00:00	Sum of Bed	0	
12			Sum of Wardrobe	2	
13			Sum of Drawers	2	
14			Sum of CoffeeTable	0	
15			Sum of Kitchen	5	
16			Sum of Chair	0	
17			Sum of Table	0	
18	05/02/2000	05/02/2000 00:00	Sum of Bed	2	
19			Sum of Wardrobe	2	

6. Save your workbook.

Over to you: mandatory

The PivotTable now displays sales totals for each furniture type for January as a whole, then for all other dates in the year individually.

Next, you will finish grouping the PivotTable data and add the results you calculate to MFPF_FINANCE.XLS (or Ex5.4-MFPF_FINANCE.xls).

- Group the dates for each of the other months together, hide the details in the *OrderDate* field, and rename the groups.
  You can do this using Excel's automatic grouping function if you prefer, but you'll need to ungroup the January dates again first.
- Finally, copy the monthly totals into the space left for them on the *SALES TOTALS* worksheet in the MFPF_FINANCE.XLS (or Ex5.4-MFPF_FINANCE.xls) workbook. You will need to use **Edit | Paste Special** to paste the values and transpose them.

Save both workbooks when you are done.

Refresh PivotTables

In *Chapter 3: Importing data into a spreadsheet* on page 15, you learned that you could update data imported from a delimited text file or from a database to match the source data at any time.

You can also refresh PivotTables so that they reflect the most current data in the data source defined.

In the next exercise, you will make a change to the sales data on the *COMPLETE* worksheet of MFPF_ORD.XLS (or Ex7.2-OTYM1-MFPF_ORD.xls) and refresh your PivotTable to see this.

Don't worry – if you manually change the information on the *COMPLETE* worksheet, you won't affect the database the results came from: you can simply refresh your data any time, and the values will change back to match those in the database again.

Exercise 7.3: Updating the data in a PivotTable

1. Go to the *COMPLETE* worksheet of MFPF_ORD.XLS (or Ex7.2-OTYM1-MFPF_ORD.xls).
   Change any one of the orders to include a request for 2000 wardrobes.
2. Go to the *PIVOT* worksheet.
3. Select **Data | Refresh Data**.
4. Look for the total that has been affected by the change you made. A month with in excess of 2000 wardrobe orders is easy to find!

Over to you: optional

Experiment with creating PivotTables to summarize the data on the *COMPLETE* worksheet of MFPF_ORD.XLS (or Ex7.3-MFPF_ORD.xls).

Here are some ideas for reports you could generate:

- A report showing the average order by a given customer for each furniture type in a year
- A report showing the largest orders for specific furniture types by each company
- A report showing the total sales of each furniture type in specific towns

Try grouping the furniture types in each of the reports according to whether items are intended for indoor or outdoor use and look for trends in purchasing patterns.

Chapter summary

A PivotTable is an interactive table that allows you to dynamically create reports summarizing large amounts of data.

PivotTables can be based on data from databases or from Excel spreadsheets.

A field in a PivotTable corresponds to a column in the data source that the PivotTable is based on.

You can group fields in a PivotTable to make it easier to view or select subsets of records. A group is a set of objects that is treated as a single object.

PivotTables can be refreshed at any time to reflect changes in their data source.

Quick Quiz

Circle the answer to each of the following multiple-choice questions about PivotTables.

Q1	A PivotTable allows you to summarize data from... (Circle all that apply.)
A.	Spreadsheets.
B.	Text files.
C.	Word documents.
D.	Databases.

Q2	If the source data changes, you can update a PivotTable based on the data using Refresh Data.
A.	True.
B.	False.

Q3	Fields in PivotTables refer to what in the source data?
A.	Rows.
B.	Columns.
C.	Cells.
D.	Worksheet names.

Q4	You can group data in PivotTables...
A.	By date.
B.	Alphabetically.
C.	According to any system you want.
D.	All of the above.

Q5	Once data has been grouped, you can't ungroup it again.
A.	True.
B.	False.

Answers   **1:** A, D; **2:** A; **3:** B; **4:** D; **5:** B.

Chapter 8: Linking to data in spreadsheets

In this chapter

In *Chapter 6* you created a link from one cell to the value in another using **Paste Special**. In this chapter you will find out how to create links between cells by manually entering link formulae.

You will also see how Excel charts remain linked to their source data, and how changes in the source values are automatically reflected in the charts.

Finally, you will learn how to add a link from a Word document to a cell range in an Excel spreadsheet.

New skills

At the end of this chapter you should be able to:

- Create links to cells on the same worksheet
- Create links to cells on other worksheets
- Create links to cells in other workbooks
- Add a chart linked to a cell range in one worksheet to any worksheet or workbook
- Create links from Word to cells in an Excel spreadsheet

New words

There are no new words in this chapter.

Syllabus reference

The following syllabus items are covered in this chapter:
- AM 4.2.3.1 – Link data / chart within a worksheet.
- AM 4.2.3.2 – Link data / chart between worksheets.
- AM 4.2.3.3 – Link data / chart between spreadsheets.
- AM 4.2.3.4 – Link data / chart into a word processing document.

Linking to a cell on the same worksheet

You have used formulae in Excel before to perform calculations.

For example, the formula =*SUM(A1:A12)* uses the SUM function to add together the values in each cell in the range *A1:A12*, and displays the result.

When you create a link from one cell to another in an Excel spreadsheet, you use a link formula to refer to a cell's contents.

To create a link from one cell on a worksheet to another, you use a link formula in the form =*cellname* – for example, =*A1*.

If you had named the cell, you could refer to it by this custom name instead – for example =*CustomName1*. The result would be the same: the value shown in the cell containing the link is the same value displayed in the linked cell.

> **Note:** As with links created using **Paste Special**, if you change the position of the referred cell (source) or referring cell (destination), the link is updated to reflect the change.

In the next exercise, you will link a cell on the *OUTGOING* worksheet of MFPF_FINANCE.XLS (or Ex7.2-OTYM2-MFPF_FINANCE.xls) to another cell on the same worksheet.

Exercise 8.1: Linking cells on a worksheet

1. Open MFPF_FINANCE.XLS (or Ex7.2-OTYM2-MFPF_FINANCE.xls) and go to the *OUTGOING* worksheet.
2. In cell *A17*, enter the label *Outgoing total*.
3. In cell *C17*, enter the link formula =*C15*.
   Cell *C17* is now linked to the value in cell *C15*.
4. Enter number values in blank cells in the *Petrol* column and observe that the numbers in cells *C15* and *C17* both change.

Linking to cells in other worksheets

To create a link from a cell in one worksheet to a cell in another worksheet, you use the same principle, but you add an extra piece of information to your link formula which tells Excel which worksheet in the current workbook to look at.

A link from a cell in one worksheet to a cell in another worksheet in the same workbook is in the form =*sheetname!cellname* – for example, =*Sheet1!A1*.

A cell can have a default name and any number of custom names at the same time. A worksheet can only have one name, and this must be the name used in the link formula.

> **Note:** If you change the name of a worksheet *after* creating a link to a cell on that worksheet, the link formula will automatically update to reflect the new worksheet name. However, if you change the worksheet name first, then try to link to its original name, that won't work: if *Sheet1* becomes *MyFavouriteWorksheet*, Excel forgets it ever used to be called *Sheet1*!

In the next exercise, you will create a link on the *PROFIT* worksheet of MFPF_FINANCE.XLS (or Ex8.1-MFPF_FINANCE.xls) to the cell containing the value for total annual outgoings on the *OUTGOING* worksheet.

Exercise 8.2: Linking cells across worksheets

1. Go to the *PROFIT* worksheet of MFPF_FINANCE.XLS (or Ex8.1-MFPF_FINANCE.xls).
2. In cell *A17*, enter the label *Outgoing Total*.
3. In cell *C17*, enter the link formula =*OUTGOING!C17*.
   Cell *C17* is now linked to cell *C17* of the *OUTGOING* worksheet in the same workbook.
4. Delete the entries you added in the *Petrol* column on the *OUTGOING* worksheet in *Exercise 8.1* on page 86.
   The contents of cells *C15* and *C17* on the *OUTGOING* worksheet, and those of cell *C17* on the *PROFIT* sheet update automatically to reflect your changes.

Linking to cells in other workbooks

You can even create a link from a cell in one workbook to a cell in another workbook. The link formula is in the form *=[bookname]sheetname!cellname* – for example, *=[book1.xls]sheet1!A1*.

Note: If both workbooks are in the same folder, you only need to give the filename in the square brackets. If the files are in different folders you will need to enter the full path, including filename, between the square brackets in the link formula.

Note: Excel automatically keeps track of changes to worksheet and even workbook names in cross-workbook links, *provided* both the linked to and linking workbooks are both open when you make the changes! If you change the source workbook or worksheet name while the linking workbook is closed, you will have to fix the broken link formulae manually when you reopen the file.

Exercise 8.3: Linking cells across workbooks

1. Add a new worksheet to MFPF_FINANCE.XLS (or Ex8.2-MFPF_FINANCE.xls).
2. In cell *A1* on the new worksheet, enter the link
   =[MFPF_ORD.xls]OUTDOOR!$A$1
   The value in cell *A1* on the *OUTDOOR* worksheet of MFPF_ORD.XLS now appears in cell *A1* of the new worksheet.
3. Delete the added worksheet, and save your workbook.

Cell references in formulae

The format used in link formulae to refer to cells in other worksheets and workbooks can be used in other formulae too.

For example, the following formula adds the contents of cell *A1* on *sheet1* of the current workbook to the contents of cell *A1* on *sheet1* of a workbook called book1.xls:
=sheet1!A1+[book1.xls]sheet1!A1.

Linking to cells in Excel workbooks from Word

Using Word's **Paste Special** command, you can create a link from a Word document to a cell range in an Excel workbook.

When you change the data in the Excel spreadsheet, the linked cell range in the Word document is automatically updated to reflect your changes. As with cross-workbook links, if you change the name of the linked workbook or any of the worksheets or cells in the workbook while the Word document containing the link is open, the link will automatically update to reflect the name changes. *However*, if you change the *locations* of any of the cells referred to, Word will continue to show to the original cell range specified regardless.

Mr Murphy is applying for a business loan to buy new machinery for the warehouse. He has already been to see the local bank manager who has asked to see a summary of the business's incomings and outgoings for the previous year before agreeing to the loan. You have been asked to add these details to a letter Mr Murphy has written.

Although you have not yet calculated the final figures in MFPF_FINANCE.XLS, you *do* know which cell range they will go in. You can add a link to the relevant cell range now, and then when you're finished making your calculations, all you will need to do is open the letter and print it. The data from the cell range in the workbook will be filled into the letter automatically.

In the next exercise you will add a link from a letter written in Word to a cell range in the *PROFIT* worksheet of MFPF_FINANCE.XLS (or Ex8.2-MFPF_FINANCE.xls).

Exercise 8.4: Linking from Word to cells in a spreadsheet

1. Go to the *PROFIT* worksheet of MFPF_FINANCE.XLS (or Ex8.2-MFPF_FINANCE.xls).
2. Copy the cell range *A1:D15*.
3. Open the Word document LETTER.DOC, and go to the empty paragraph after the line 'I trust they will be to your satisfaction.'
4. Select **Edit | Paste Special** in Word.
   The *Paste Special* dialog box opens.

5. Select *Paste link*, then select *MS Excel Worksheet Object* (*Microsoft Office Excel Worksheet Object* in Word 2003) from the *As* area.

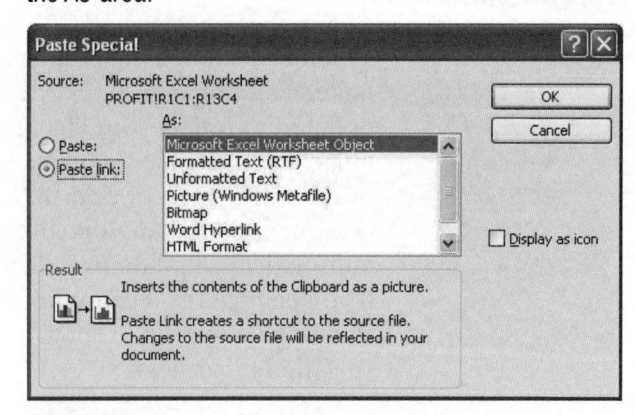

Click **OK**.
A link is added from the Word document to the copied cells in the Excel spreadsheet.
Your letter should now look like this:

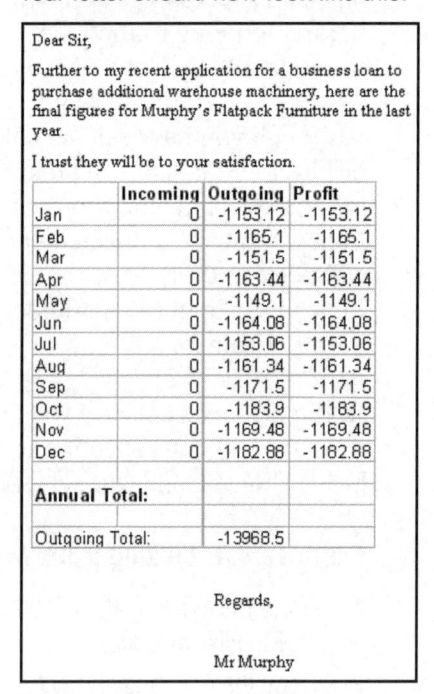

6. Save and close LETTER.DOC when you are done.

Note: You can create a link from a Word document to an Excel chart in exactly the same way, for example to display the monthly Incomings, Outgoings and Profits in a bar chart.

Chapter 8: Linking to data in spreadsheets

Over to you: optional

Next, you will check that the link you created from the Word document to the Excel worksheet cell range really works.

- Add some numbers to the *INCOMING* and *OUTGOING* columns in the *PROFIT* worksheet in MFPF_FINANCE.XLS. Open LETTER.DOC and check that the cells in the Word document have been updated to reflect your changes. Delete the numbers you added to the *PROFIT* worksheet when you are done.

Linking charts

When you create a chart in Excel, it is automatically linked to the source data from which it was generated. When you edit the source data, the chart automatically updates to reflect your changes. Also, as with other links in Excel, if the locations of the source cells change, the chart updates its references to link to the new locations.

When you create a chart, you are given the option of adding it to the current worksheet or to a new worksheet in the same workbook. To add the chart to a different worksheet in the current workbook, or to a worksheet in a different workbook, you must use **Copy** and **Paste**. Copies of the chart also remain linked to the source data.

In the following exercise you will create a chart which shows MFPF's monthly telephone bill expenditure.

Exercise 8.5: Creating a linked chart

1. Go to the *OUTGOING* worksheet of MFPF_FINANCE.XLS (or Ex8.4-MFPF_FINANCE.xls).
2. Select the non-adjacent cell ranges *A2:A13* and *D2:D13*. (To select non-adjacent cell ranges, select the first range, then holding down the **CTRL** key, select the second range.)
3. Select **Insert | Chart...**.
   – or –
   Click the **Chart Wizard** button on the *Standard* toolbar.
   The *Chart Wizard* opens.
4. In the *Chart Wizard*, select *Column* in the *Chart type* field and click **Finish**.

Chart Wizard button

5. A column chart indicating how much was spent on the telephone bill each month is inserted into the current worksheet.

In the next exercise, you will add copies of the chart you just created to a new worksheet in MFPF_FINANCE.XLS (or Ex8.5-MFPF_FINANCE.xls), to a worksheet in a new workbook, and to a Word document. You will then edit the value of the phone bill for one month and see all of the chart copies update to reflect that change.

Exercise 8.6: Creating copies of a linked chart

1. Select the chart you created in the last exercise.
2. Select **Edit | Copy**.
3. Select **Insert | Worksheet** to add a new worksheet to MFPF_FINANCE.XLS (or Ex8.5-MFPF_FINANCE.xls).
4. Open the new worksheet and select **Edit | Paste**.
5. Select **File | New...** and create a new workbook based on the default template.
6. In the new workbook, paste the copied chart to the *Sheet1* worksheet in the new workbook.
7. Start Microsoft Word and create a new blank document.
8. In Word, select **Edit | Paste Special...**, select to paste a link to the copied chart in the new blank document and click **OK**.
9. Change the entry in cell *D3* on the *OUTGOING* worksheet in MFPF_FINANCE.XLS (or Ex8.5-MFPF_FINANCE.xls) to –10 and press **ENTER**.
   The copies of the chart that you pasted to Excel spreadsheets update automatically to reflect the change.
   To update the chart in the Word document, you will need to right-click the chart and click **Update Link** in the pop-up menu that appears.

Close all your workbooks *without saving* when you are done.

Chapter summary

You can create a link from a cell in an Excel spreadsheet to any other cell in any worksheet in any workbook. The complete format for such links is
=*[bookname]sheetname!cellname* – for example,
=*[Book1.xls]Sheet1!A1*.

If you change workbook, worksheet or cell names, or even cell locations, Excel automatically updates any links in your workbooks *provided* both the source and destination workbooks are open at the time you make your changes.

Charts created in Excel are automatically linked to the source data they were generated from. Even if a chart is copied to another worksheet or workbook, it remains linked to its source data and updates automatically to reflect changes in that data.

You can use Word's **Paste Special** command to create a link from a Word document to a cell range or chart in an Excel workbook. If the values in the cell range change, the values in the Word document update to reflect the changes.

Unlike Excel links, Word links will update to reflect changes to workbook and worksheet names, but not changes to cell locations. Again, both the workbook(s) with the linked cells and the Word document must be open when changes are made to the workbook(s).

Quick Quiz

Circle the answer to each of the following multiple-choice questions about linking to spreadsheet data.

Q1	You can link to cells in which of the following? (Circle all that apply.)
A.	The same worksheet.
B.	The same workbook.
C.	Another workbook in the same directory.
D.	A Word document.

Q2	If you change the name of a referenced cell, you must update any cross references to that cell manually...
A.	Always.
B.	If they are on a different worksheet.
C.	If they are in a different workbook.
D.	Only if the spreadsheet with the link(s) wasn't open when you changed the cell's name.

Q3	After creating a chart, you cannot edit the location of the cells the chart uses as source data.
A.	True.
B.	False.

Q4	If you change the source data used by a chart, you must recreate the chart to update it.
A.	True.
B.	False.

Q5	You can link to Excel cell ranges and charts from Word documents.
A.	True.
B.	False.

Answers   **1:** A, B, C; **2:** D; **3:** B; **4:** B; **5:** A.

Chapter 9: Formatting your spreadsheets

In this chapter

When you have added data to your spreadsheet, you will usually add some formatting to make the information clearer and easier on the eye.

In ECDL 3 or ECDL 4 you learned how to apply text and number formats to cells in an Excel spreadsheet.

In this chapter you will learn about other more advanced formatting options in Excel.

New skills

At the end of this chapter you should be able to:

- Freeze row and column titles
- Use Excel's AutoFormat option
- Create and apply a custom number format
- Use conditional formatting

New words

There are no new words in this chapter.

Syllabus reference

The following syllabus items are covered in this chapter:
- AM 4.1.1.2 – Apply automatic formatting to a cell range.
- AM 4.1.1.3 – Create custom number formats.
- AM 4.1.1.4 – Use conditional formatting options.
- AM 4.1.2.1 – Freeze row and/or column titles.

Freezing row and column titles

Where a spreadsheet contains many rows and columns, you may find that when you scroll down or across the worksheet, you are looking at a part of the spreadsheet where no row or column labels are visible. Unless the information in each column is very distinctive, for example, Name, Address and Telephone Number, the data may be difficult to read – if there are lots and lots of currency values, how do you know which ones refer to telephone bills, which to electricity, or which ones are totals or averages of other values?

As an example, open MFPF_ORD.XLS (or Ex7.3-MFPF_ORD.xls), go to the *COMPLETE* worksheet, type *H50* into the *Name* box and press **Enter** to go to cell *H50*. What does the number you are looking at refer to? All the cells around it contain similar data. Unless you have a very large, high-resolution monitor, you probably cannot see the column label for this cell when you're looking at it.

To determine what the number in the cell you are looking at refers to, you could scroll to the top of the sheet to see the column label and then scroll back again, and that's an easy enough thing to do when you're only on row 50, but what if you were on row 5000? Wouldn't it be nice to be able to see the column labels all the time, no matter how far down the spreadsheet you scrolled?

Well, you can. Excel allows you to select a row, or set of rows, at the top of a spreadsheet and 'freeze' them in place so that you can see them no matter how far down the rest of the sheet you scroll. You can also freeze a column, or group of columns, at the left of the spreadsheet to have permanently visible row labels. When freezing rows and columns, remember that less is more – if you freeze too many labels, you may wind up with so little screen left over that you can only scroll through your labelled data a couple of records at a time!

In the next exercise, you will create frozen column and row titles on the *COMPLETE* worksheet of MFPF_ORD.XLS (or Ex7.3-MFPF_ORD.xls).

Exercise 9.1: Freezing row and column titles

1. Open MFPF_ORD.XLS (or Ex7.3-MFPF_ORD.xls) and go to the *COMPLETE* worksheet.

Vertical split box →

2. Click and drag the vertical split box, located at the top of the vertical scroll bar, to just below row 1.
   The column titles are separated from the rest of the spreadsheet.

Horizontal split box

3. Click and drag the horizontal split box, located at the right of the horizontal scroll bar, to the right of column *B*.
   The cells containing the *OrderDate* and *CompanyName* for each row are separated from the rest of the spreadsheet.
   Your worksheet should now look like as follows:

	A	B	C	D	E	F	G
1	OrderDate	CompanyName	Town	Wardrobe	Bed	Drawers	CoffeeT
2	05-01-00 0:00	Joe's Hardware	Cullenstown	6	4	8	
3	05-02-00 0:00	Joe's Hardware	Cullenstown	2	2	4	
4	05-03-00 0:00	Joe's Hardware	Cullenstown	0	0	5	
5	05-04-00 0:00	Joe's Hardware	Cullenstown	4	0	5	
6	05-05-00 0:00	Joe's Hardware	Cullenstown	4	0	4	
7	05-06-00 0:00	Joe's Hardware	Cullenstown	0	0	6	
8	05-07-00 0:00	Joe's Hardware	Cullenstown	0	4	0	
9	05-08-00 0:00	Joe's Hardware	Cullenstown	0	4	10	
10	05-10-00 0:00	Joe's Hardware	Cullenstown	0	0	0	
11	05-11-00 0:00	Joe's Hardware	Cullenstown	4	4	12	
12	05-12-00 0:00	Joe's Hardware	Cullenstown	0	0	2	
13	26-05-00 0:00	Cullenstown Garden Centre	Cullenstown	0	0	0	

With the worksheet divided in this way, you can scroll in each quadrant independently.

4. Select **Window | Freeze panes**.
   The split dividers disappear, and are replace by lines.
   You can now only scroll in the lower left quadrant.

5. Scroll down the worksheet. The frozen column titles remain visible no matter which rows you are looking at.
   Next, scroll across the worksheet. The frozen cells indicating the *OrderDate* and *CompanyName* for each order remain visible no matter which columns you are looking at.

6. Save and close your workbook when you are done.

You can unfreeze areas by selecting **Window | Unfreeze Panes**. Then, to get rid of the split entirely, select **Window | Remove Split**.

Note: If you want to freeze both horizontal *and* vertical portions of the screen, you must add *both* splits before freezing. Once a window has been frozen, you cannot split it again. Also, you can only make one split in each direction.

Note: You can also freeze by selecting the cell below the row(s) and to the right of the column(s) you want to freeze, but it's easier to see what the end result will be if you apply a split first.

Using AutoFormat

When you apply formatting to a spreadsheet, you can spend a lot of time deciding how you want your data to look, and then applying different fill colours, fonts, etc.

Excel's **AutoFormat** facility allows you to select one of 17 pre-defined design schemes and apply it to a cell range. Each scheme defines formats for numbers, borders, fonts, patterns, alignment, and cell width and height.

In the next exercise, you will format the accounting information on the *OUTGOING* worksheet of MFPF_FINANCE.XLS (or Ex8.6-MFPF_FINANCE.xls) using an Excel **AutoFormat** option.

Exercise 9.2: Applying AutoFormat

1. Open MFPF_FINANCE.XLS (or Ex8.6-MFPF_FINANCE.xls) and go to the *OUTGOING* worksheet.
2. Select the cell range *A1:G15*.
3. Select **Format | AutoFormat...**.
   The *AutoFormat* dialog box opens.
   A sample of each format you can apply is shown in the left-hand panel of the dialog box, with its name below it.
4. Select the style *Classic3* by clicking it once.
   A black border appears around the format to indicate that it has been selected.
5. Click **Options...**.
   The *Formats to apply* area opens at the bottom of the dialog box where you can specify a subset of the format elements of the format you want to use.

[AutoFormat dialog box image]

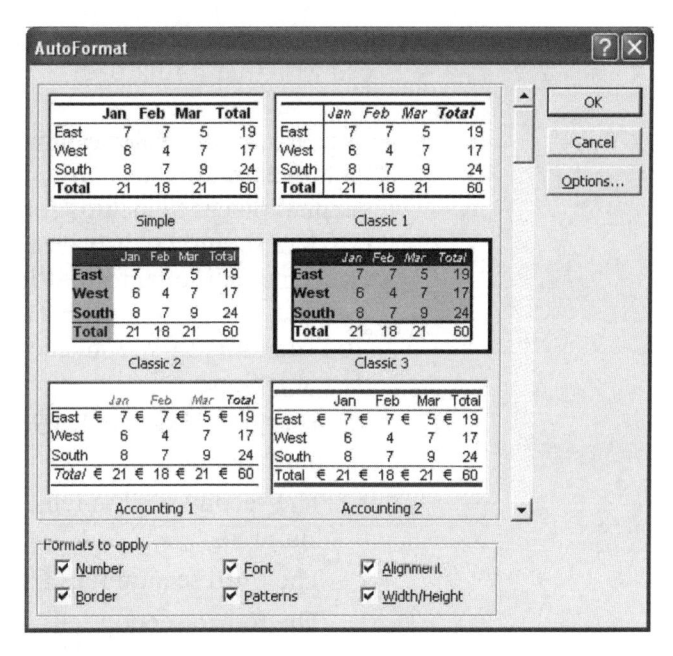

Deselect the *Border* option.
Each format preview changes to show how the format looks without borders.

6. Click **OK**.
The *Classic3* format is applied to the cell range *A1:G15* on the *OUTGOING* worksheet.

7. Save your workbook when you are done.

Over to you: optional

Try applying other **AutoFormat** styles to the cell range you just formatted. When you find one you like, apply the same format to the accounting information on the *INCOMING* and *PROFIT* worksheets.

Custom number formats

In ECDL 3 or ECDL 4 you learned how to apply number formats to cells in a worksheet to define how numeric data should appear. For example, with a certain number of decimal places, with a particular thousands indicator, or with a particular currency symbol.

If you want to use a number format that doesn't already exist in Excel, you can define a custom number format by opening the *Format Cells* dialog box, going to the *Number* tab and entering the appropriate format code(s) under *Custom*.

Format codes tell Excel how to format the data entered in a cell with that formatting.

Your formatting rules can include specifications for how to handle dates, text or numeric data. For example, how many decimal places to include for numerical data, what colour the data should be displayed in, any text to append/prepend or even conditional formatting rules to apply.

You can enter up to four sections of format codes, separated by semicolons:

- The first section tells Excel how to format positive numbers.
- The second section tells Excel how to format negative numbers.
- The third section tells Excel how to format zero values.
- The fourth section tells Excel how to format text.

You don't have to specify all four sections: you can skip a section by leaving it blank and entering its closing semicolon before defining the next section.

Alternatively, you can specify only one or two sections: if you specify only one, Excel uses that format for all data entered in the cell you apply the formatting to; if you specify two, Excel uses the first section to format positive numbers and zeros and the second to format negative numbers.

The complete list of formatting rules is too extensive to cover here in detail: for full details of all the format codes available in Excel, refer to Excel's online help. Some common formatting codes you may want to use are described here:

- The code # tells Excel to display a numeric digit, if there is one to display. For example, the format code: #,###.# tells Excel to display numbers entered into the formatted cell to one decimal place and with a comma as a thousands separator. If the entered number goes to more than one decimal place, Excel will round and truncate the number for display. However, with this code, if the number has no decimal places, it will terminate with the decimal point itself. Try it and see.

- The code 0 tells Excel to display a numeric digit, if there is one to display, or *0* if there isn't. For example, the format code #00.0 tells Excel to display numbers entered into the formatted cell with at least two digits before the decimal point and one digit after the decimal place, even if that digit is 0.
- Colour format codes can be used to tell Excel to format data in a particular colour. For example, the format code #.0;[Red]#.0 tells Excel to format positive numbers in the default font colour with one digit after the decimal point, and negative numbers in red with one digit after the decimal point.
- You could combine the formats in the last example by specifying a conditional format code. For example, the format code [Red][<0]#.00 tells Excel to format numbers with two digits after the decimal point and negative numbers additionally in red.
- You can add text to a format by entering it in the format description in inverted commas. For example, the format code ##.00"cm" tells Excel to display numbers entered in the formatted cell with at least two digits after the decimal point and the text *cm* immediately after the number.

If you want to create a custom format that is similar to an existing format, you can select the existing format and copy its definition to use as a basis for your new custom format.

> **Note:** Remember that you are allowed to refer to Excel's online help during the ECDL exam, so you can check the details of how to specify format codes when you create a custom number format – you don't need to learn the codes off by heart!

Mr Murphy has asked you to format numbers in a cell range in DELIVERIES.XLS (or Ex3.2-OTYM1-DELIVERIES.xls) as distances in kilometres. There is no default number style in Excel that will let you do this. If you just added the letters *km* to the numbers in each cell, the cell contents would be treated as text, and you would not be able to use the data in calculations later.

In the next exercise you will create a custom number format to indicate kilometre distances, and apply it to a cell range.

Exercise 9.3: Creating a custom number format

1. Open DELIVERIES.XLS (or Ex3.2-OTYM1-DELIVERIES.xls) and go to the *CHARGES* worksheet.
2. Select column *B*, which lists the distances to each customer's premises.
3. Select **Format | Cells...**.
   The *Format Cells* dialog box opens.

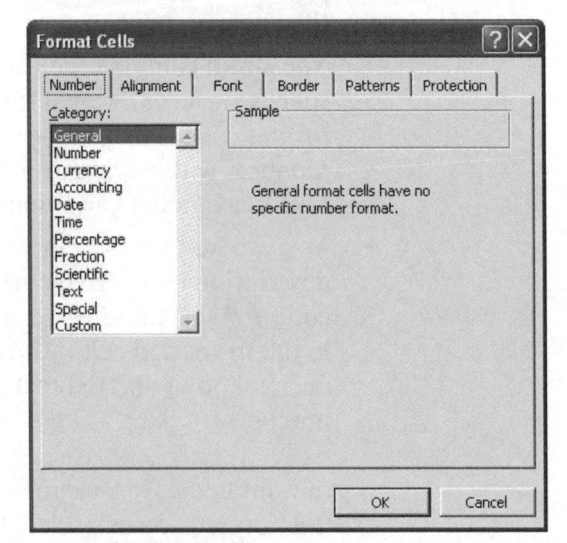

4. Click the **Number** tab.
5. Select *Custom* in the *Category* list.
6. In the *Type* field enter the text *0.0 "km"* (including the quotation marks) and press **Enter**.
   All the cells in column *B* which contain numeric data are now formatted to have one decimal place, and the letters *km* appear after the numbers.
7. Save and close your workbook when you are done.

Conditional formatting

Sometimes you will want to apply a certain type of formatting to data only if they satisfy certain criteria. For example, you might want to format every negative number in a cell range in bold red text.

You could look at the values in each cell, identify the negative ones, and manually apply the required formatting to each one. Alternatively, you could use conditional formatting to automatically check the values in each cell of a cell range, and format the negative ones in bold red text.

You can also format the contents of one cell in a particular way if the value in a different cell satisfies certain criteria.

For example, in cell *D9* on the *Personal Notes* worksheet of INVOICE_MFPF.XLT, the text *Late* has been entered and formatted in white so that it cannot be seen. The cell has conditional formatting associated with it: if the payment date in cell *C9* is more than 28 days after the invoice date in cell *C8*, the text in this cell is formatted in red and becomes visible.

MFPF have estimated ideal maximum payments for each utility. The estimated maximum for any electricity bill is £40. You have been asked to automatically flag any bill that exceeds that amount.

In the next exercise, you will apply conditional formatting to data in the *Electricity* column on the *OUTGOING* worksheet of MFPF_FINANCE.XLS (or Ex9.2-MFPF_FINANCE.xls), so that any payment exceeding £40 is shown in bold red text.

Exercise 9.4: Applying conditional formatting

1. Go to the *OUTGOING* worksheet of MFPF_FINANCE.XLS (or Ex9.2-MFPF_FINANCE.xls).
2. Select the cell range *C2:C13* which contains the values for electricity payments made by the business.
3. Select **Format | Conditional Formatting...**.
   The *Conditional Formatting* dialog box opens.
4. In the *Condition 1* area of the *Conditional Formatting* dialog box, set the following condition:
   Cell Value Is less than or equal to − 40.
   Remember, because the numbers on this worksheet indicate money that is being paid out by the business, they have been entered as negative values.

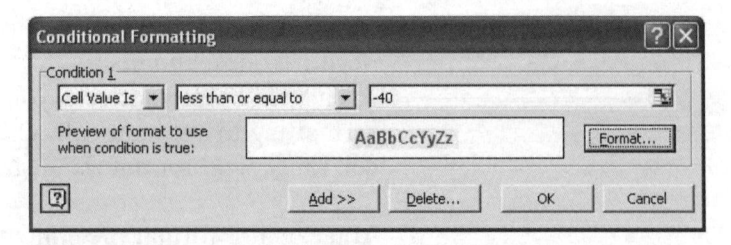

[Screenshot of Conditional Formatting dialog box showing Condition 1 with "Cell Value Is" "less than or equal to" "-40", and a preview of format AaBbCcYyZz]

5. Click **Format...** to open the *Format Cells* dialog box where you will specify the format to apply if the condition is met.
6. In the *Format Cells* dialog box, select *Bold* in the *Font Style* area, and *Red* in the *Color* drop-down list.
   Click **OK**.
   You could add more conditional formatting rules to the cell by clicking **Add**. For now, you will only apply one conditional format.
7. Click **OK**.
8. Save your workbook.

The value in cell *C3* is now formatted in bold red text, as it exceeds the estimated maximum, as defined in *Condition 1*.

Over to you: optional

To impress the Murphys, you decide in addition to flag entries where the payment amount is very close to the estimated maximum.

- Append additional conditional formatting rules to the one you created in the last exercise to format payments of £39 and over in bold orange text, and those of £38 and over in bold yellow text.

  Note: Excel applies formatting to the contents of a cell according to which of the defined conditions is satisfied first. This means that the order you define your conditional formatting rules in is important. £41 is obviously greater than £38, £39 and £40. If you specify the rules in the order given, £41 will be formatted in red; however if you were to specify them in the reverse order, it would be formatted in yellow.

Chapter summary

Excel allows you to select a row, or set of rows, at the top of a spreadsheet and 'freeze' them so that you can see them no matter how far down the rest of the sheet you scroll. You can also freeze a column or group of columns at the left of the spreadsheet to have permanently visible row labels.

Excel's **AutoFormat** facility allows you to select one of 17 pre-defined design schemes and apply it to a cell range. Each scheme defines formats for numbers, borders, fonts, patterns, alignment, and cell width and height.

You can define custom number formats to use when formatting cells in Excel.

You can also use conditional formatting rules to format data in a certain way if they satisfy specified criteria.

Quick Quiz

Circle the answer to each of the following multiple-choice questions about formatting spreadsheets.

Q1	Which of the following statements about freezing rows and columns is *true*?
A.	You can freeze rows and columns at the same time.
B.	You must always freeze rows before freezing columns.
C.	You can apply up to 3 splits in each direction.
D.	You can continue to freeze columns after you have finished freezing rows, and vice versa.

Q2	If you freeze rows and columns on one worksheet in a workbook, the same rows and columns are frozen on all other worksheets in the same workbook.
A.	True.
B.	False.

Q3	You can choose to apply only subsets of the format elements in predefined AutoFormats.
A.	True.
B.	False.

Q4	If you type a unit, such a currency symbol or distance label, with the numeric value in a cell, can the number still be used in calculations?
A.	Yes.
B.	No.

Q5	In which order are conditional formatting rules read?
A.	First to last.
B.	Last to first.
C.	In ascending order of the value to compare to.
D.	In descending order of the value to compare to.

Answers **1:** A; **2:** B; **3:** A; **4:** B; **5:** A.

Chapter 10: Using Excel macros

In this chapter

Excel allows you to save time on repetitive tasks in several ways.

Earlier, you learned how to use a template to save default content and settings for a type of spreadsheet you would use many times.

In this chapter, you will learn the equally useful skill of defining your own commands in Excel to perform any series of actions that you repeat regularly.

New skills

At the end of this chapter you should be able to:

- Record a macro
- Run a recorded macro
- Assign a recorded macro to a toolbar button

New words

At the end of this chapter you should be able to explain the following terms:

- Macro

Syllabus reference

The following syllabus items are covered in this chapter:
- AM 4.5.1.1 – Record a simple macro (e.g. page setup changes.)
- AM 4.5.1.2 – Run a macro.
- AM 4.5.1.3 – Assign a macro to a custom button on a toolbar.

What are macros?

From time to time, you will want to perform the same series of actions on a cell or cell range in several worksheets or even workbooks.

For example, say you use Excel to keep track of all the phone calls you make in a month. Each month you create a new worksheet and enter the numbers you dial in column *A* and the call durations in column *B*. At the end of the month, you sort the entries on the sheet by the number dialled, then apply text formatting to column *A* and numeric formatting, including showing a currency symbol, to column *B*. You apply conditional formatting to column *B*, to highlight any calls that went on for over an hour, and conditional formatting to column *A* to pick out which numbers don't belong to close friends or family.

Because you perform these exact actions in exactly the same way every month, it would save you *lots* of time in the long run to have a single Excel command that could perform this task for you.

Well, believe it or not, you *can* create a command that performs all of these actions, and save it in Excel!

Excel allows you to record a series of actions which are always performed in the same way, and in the same order, and save them as a new command, called a macro.

Macro
A macro is a custom command defined to perform a series of specific actions in the same way and in the same order every time the macro is run.

Macros are associated with Excel workbooks. You can save a macro in one of three places:

- Personal Macro Workbook – The Personal Macro Workbook is stored in the Excel startup folder. Any macros you save in this workbook will be available to you whenever you run Excel, no matter what workbook you are editing.

- New Workbook – You can choose to create a new workbook and save the macro there. The macro will be available to you when you edit the new workbook.
- This Workbook – If you save the macro in the workbook you create it in, it will be available to you whenever you edit that workbook.

Note: If a workbook you open contains macros, a dialog box will appear alerting you to this fact, and asking if you want to enable or disable the macros. If you disable the macros, they cannot run. This allows you to protect yourself from viruses written as Excel macros.

Recording macros

To record a macro in Excel, you first tell Excel to start recording what you are doing, then you perform the actions you want the macro to perform whenever you run it. When you have finished, you tell Excel to stop recording your actions. Everything you do from the time you tell Excel to start recording to when you tell it to stop is included in the macro.

If you apply formatting to a cell, then change your mind and change it to something else, both of the formatting actions are remembered and performed, in the same order, by the macro when it is run. Every action included in the macro increases its size, so you must be clear before you start recording exactly what it is that you want to record.

Note: If you know how to program in Visual Basic (VB), you can create or tweak macros by editing them in Excel's Visual Basic Editor, accessed by clicking **Tools | Macro | Visual Basic Editor**. This would allow you to remove such accidental extra steps without having to rerecord the entire macro from scratch.

Another important aspect of macros is that they can be *absolute* or *relative*.

Absolute macros

An absolute macro is one that performs the exact same set of actions on the exact same cell or cell range whenever it is run. An absolute macro might always change the format for columns *A* and *D*, or always delete the contents of the cell range *A3:D5*, for example.

Relative macros

A relative macro performs the set of recorded actions relative to the cell or cell range selected when you run the macro. A relative macro might assign a particular background colour, text colour, font and number format to the contents of the selected cell or cell range when it is run, for example.

Mr Murphy urgently needs the *COMPLETE*, *INDOOR* and *OUTDOOR* worksheets of MFPF_ORD.XLS (or Ex9.1-MFPF_ORD.xls) reformatted. He has asked you to apply a certain type of formatting to all three sheets in the next 5 minutes.

You know that you can apply the required formatting to one of the sheets in 5 minutes, but doubt you'll have time to format the other two sheets as well. But, if you record the changes you make to the first sheet in a macro, then you can reapply all of the changes to each of the other sheets in seconds!

In the next exercise, you will record an absolute macro to apply formatting to data imported using the MFPF_Q1.DQY query you created and saved earlier (or Ex3.2-MFPF_Q1.dqy from the CD).

> **Note:** Before recording a macro in Excel, ensure your security level is set to either *medium* or *low*. To do this, click **Tools | Options** to open the *Options* dialog box, go to the *Security* tab, click **Macro Security** and on the *Security Level* tab of the dialog that opens, select the security level you want to use.

Exercise 10.1: Recording a macro

1. Open MFPF_ORD.XLS (or Ex9.1-MFPF_ORD.xls) and go to the *COMPLETE* worksheet.
2. In your new macro, you will include commands to split and freeze the first row and first two columns of the selected worksheet.

Before you can do this, you'll need to remove the freezes already applied to the data in the *COMPLETE* worksheet: to do this, select **Window | Unfreeze panes**, then select **Window | Remove Split**.

Now you are ready to start recording your macro.

3. Select **Tools | Macros | Record New Macro...**.
   The *Record Macro* dialog box opens.

4. In the *Macro name* field, enter *format_worksheet*.
   In the *Shortcut key* field enter *d*.
   In the *Store macro in* field, select *This Workbook*.
   In the *Description* field enter the text *Applies layout and formatting to a worksheet*.

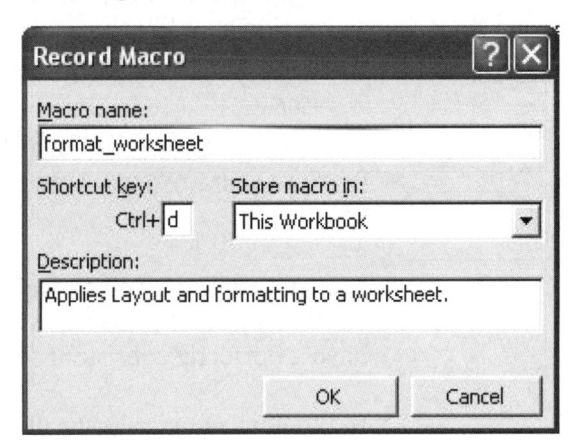

   Click **OK**.
   The *Record Macro* dialog box closes, and the *Stop Recording* toolbar appears.

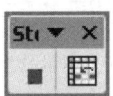

   Everything you do from now until you stop recording will be saved in the new macro.

Relative Reference button

5. You want to record an absolute macro, so make sure that the **Relative Reference** button on the *Stop Recording* toolbar is *not* pressed.
   If you wanted to record a relative macro, you would press this button first, before making any other changes you wanted to include in the macro.

6. Apply the following formatting changes:
   - Add a horizontal split below row 1
   - Add a vertical split to the right of column *B*

- Select **Window | Freeze panes**
- Format the text in row 1 as dark blue italics
- Add a background fill of pale yellow to the cells in row 1
- Format the cells in column *A* as dates, selecting *14-Mar-01* from the *Type* area on the **Number** tab of the *Format Cells* dialog box

Note: Because dates are specified in different ways in different countries, you may not see the *14-Mar-01* option listed in your default *Date Types*. If this is the case, select the *English (United States)* option from the *Locale* drop-down list below the *Types* area, and the *14-Mar-01* option should appear.

7. Select **Tools | Macro | Stop recording**.
   – or –
   Click the **Stop recording** button on the *Stop Recording* toolbar.
8. Save your workbook when you are done.

Stop Recording button

Running macros

Next, you will run your saved macro on the *INDOOR* and *OUTDOOR* worksheets and in a matter of seconds you will have a perfectly consistent set of formatted query results.

In the next exercise, you will run your macro from the *Macro* dialog box, and by using the shortcut you defined when recording the macro.

Exercise 10.2: Running a macro

1. Go to the *INDOOR* worksheet of MFPF_ORD.XLS (or Ex10.1-MFPF_ORD.xls).
2. Select **Tools | Macro | Macros...**.
   The *Macro* dialog box opens.
   This dialog box lists all of the macros saved in the current workbook.
3. Select the macro called *format_worksheet* and click **Run**.
4. Go to the *OUTDOOR* worksheet.
   Press **CTRL** and **d** to run the macro using the shortcut you defined when you created it.
5. Save your workbook when you are done.

All three worksheets are now formatted identically thanks to your macro.

Adding macros to a toolbar

You can add a custom toolbar button to any of Excel's toolbars and assign any command, including a recorded macro, to the new toolbar button.

The toolbar button will always appear on the toolbar no matter what workbook you are editing. If you click the button when you are editing a different workbook, Excel will open the workbook where the macro is saved in order to run it.

Mrs Murphy wants you to create several more worksheets containing the results of the MFPF_Q1.DQY query, with different sort and filter requirements on each. She wants to have all of the query results formatted in the same way. You decide to add a button to the *Formatting* toolbar so that you can run your macro in one click in future.

In the next exercise, you will add a new button to the *Formatting* toolbar, and assign your macro to that button.

Exercise 10.3: Assigning a macro to a toolbar button

1. Go to any worksheet in MFPF_ORD.XLS (or Ex10.2-MFPF_ORD.xls).
2. Select **View | Toolbars | Customize...**.
   The *Customize* dialog box opens.
3. Go to the **Commands** tab of the *Customize* dialog box.
4. In the *Categories* area, scroll down and select *Macros*.

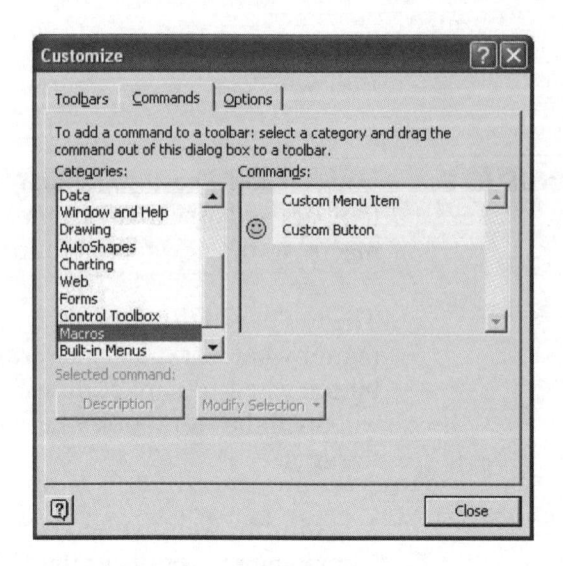

5. Click the *Custom Button* option in the *Commands* area, hold down your mouse button and drag it to the *Formatting* toolbar.
6. Right-click the new toolbar button and select *Assign Macro* from the shortcut menu that opens.
   The *Assign Macro* dialog box opens.
7. In the *Macro name* area, select *format_worksheet*, and click **OK**. 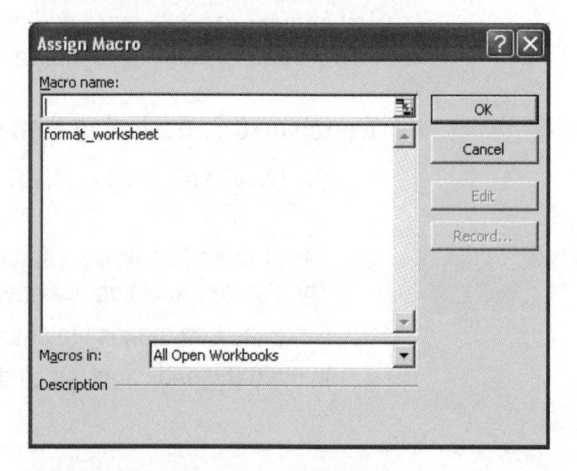
8. Click **Close** in the *Customize* dialog box.
   Your toolbar button now appears on the *Formatting* toolbar. Whenever you click it, it will run your recorded macro.
9. Save and close your workbook when you are done.

Over to you: optional

Next, you will use your new toolbar button to apply formatting to query results in a new workbook.

- Create a new workbook, run the saved query MFPF_Q1.DQY (or Ex3.2-MFPF_Q1.dqy from the CD), and click the toolbar button to run your formatting macro. Close the new workbook *without saving* when you are done.

Chapter summary

A macro is a custom command defined to perform a series of specific actions in the same way and in the same order every time the macro is run.

An absolute macro is one that performs the exact same set of actions on the exact same cell or cell range whenever it is run.

A relative macro performs the set of recorded actions relative to the cell or cell range selected when you run the macro.

You can define a shortcut when you are recording your macro, and use that shortcut to run your macro. You can also add a custom toolbar button to any Excel toolbar and assign your macro to that new toolbar button.

Quick Quiz

Circle the answer to each of the following multiple-choice questions about Excel macros.

Q1	Macros can be used to...
A.	Automatically apply formatting to data in cells.
B.	Automatically perform certain calculations.
C.	Automatically format worksheets with colours, splits, borders etc.
D.	All of the above.

Q2	A macro that acts on exactly the same cell/cells every time it is run is known as...
A.	Relative.
B.	Regular.
C.	Absolute.
D.	Abstract.

Q3	All macros are saved as part of Excel, like custom lists.
A.	True.
B.	False.

Q4	You can assign macros to toolbar buttons in Excel.
A.	True.
B.	False.

Q5	A macro will take as long to run as it took you to record it, so you must work fast when recording a macro.
A.	True.
B.	False.

Answers   **1:** D; **2:** C; **3:** B; **4:** A; **5:** B.

Chapter 11: Using reference and mathematical functions

In this chapter

Up to now, you have done a lot of work setting up your Excel spreadsheets and adding raw data to them. Now you are ready to start generating some figures for MFPF's incoming revenue and outgoing expenses in the MFPF_FINANCE.XLS workbook.

In this chapter, you will use some of Excel's mathematical functions and commands to generate these numbers.

You will also use reference functions, and learn how to nest functions.

New skills

At the end of this chapter you should be able to:

- Use HLOOKUP and VLOOKUP reference functions
- Use the **Subtotals** command
- Create a 3D SUM function
- Use the SUMIF mathematical function
- Use the ROUND mathematical function

New words

There are no new words in this chapter.

Syllabus reference

The following syllabus items are covered in this chapter:
- AM 4.1.2.4 – Use sub-totalling features.
- AM 4.2.3.5 – Consolidate data in adjacent worksheets using a 3D sum function.
- AM 4.3.1.2 – Use mathematical functions: SUMIF; SUMPOSITIVE; ROUND.
- AM 4.3.1.6 – Use lookup and reference functions: HLOOKUP; VLOOKUP.
- AM 4.3.1.9 – Use nested functions.

Maths with Paste Special

In *Chapter 6: Using Paste Special* on page 57, you learned that you can use Excel's **Paste Special** command to combine copied numerical data with numerical data in a destination cell or cell range using simple mathematical functions. Now you will use this functionality to calculate sales revenue and materials costs for the products sold by MFPF over the year.

The *INCOMING* worksheet of MFPF_FINANCE.XLS (or Ex9.4-MFPF_FINANCE.xls) has an empty column, *Products*, where you will put figures for incoming revenue from product sales.

To work out these figures, you will combine the sales figures you calculated in *Chapter 7: Summarizing data using PivotTables* on page 69, with the data you imported from PRICES.TXT in *Chapter 3: Importing data into a spreadsheet* on page 15. Both of these sets of numbers are on the *SALES TOTALS* worksheet of MFPF_FINANCE.XLS (or Ex9.4-MFPF_FINANCE.xls).

In the next exercise, you will create a copy of the named cell range *SALES*, and combine the data in the cell range with the prices in the *Sell for* row to work out the revenue generated by sales of each product each month.

Exercise 11.1: Multiplying numbers using Paste Special

1. Open MFPF_FINANCE.XLS (or Ex9.4-MFPF_FINANCE.xls) and go to the named cell range *SALES*.
2. Copy the *SALES* cell range, and paste the data to a new cell range starting in cell *A18* on the *SALES TOTALS* worksheet.
3. Name the new cell range *REVENUE*.
4. Copy the product price data in cells *B16:H16*.
5. Select the cell range *B19:H30*.
6. Select **Edit | Paste Special...**.
   The *Paste Special* dialog box opens.
7. In the *Paste* area, select *Values*.
   In the *Operations* area, select *Multiply*.
   Click **OK**.
8. Save your workbook.

The *REVENUE* cell range now indicates the total money earned by MFPF by selling each product type each month.

Over to you: mandatory

Now that you know how much was earned by selling each product type each month, you will calculate the total revenue for the month by adding up all of these figures.

- Open MFPF_FINANCE.XLS (or Ex11.1-MFPF_FINANCE.xls).

- Using the SUM function, which you learned about in ECDL 3 or ECDL 4, add up the revenue figures for all product types each month.

- Copy and paste the final revenue figures for each month into the *Products* column on the *INCOMING* worksheet.

Next you will work out how much was spent on the materials needed to make the ordered furniture each month, and add those figures to the *Raw Materials* column on the *OUTGOING* worksheet.

- Create another copy of the *SALES* range on the *SALES TOTALS* worksheet.

- Combine the data in the new cell range with the figures in the *Materials* row to calculate materials costs for each furniture type each month.

- Calculate the monthly total for materials purchases, and copy and paste the final figures to the *Raw Materials* column on the *OUTGOING* worksheet.

Save your workbook when you are done.

Reference functions

There are only two more sets of figures left to calculate to complete the records on the *INCOMING* and *OUTGOING* worksheets: revenue from delivery charges, and expenditure on petrol while making the deliveries.

To calculate these figures, you will use the data in DELIVERIES.XLS (or Ex9.3-DELIVERIES.xls). The *CHARGES* worksheet indicates how far away each customer is, and what delivery charge they pay for each order. The *DELIVERIES* worksheet lists the date of each delivery, and the customer to which the delivery was made.

You will add a third column to the *DELIVERIES* worksheet which shows the delivery charge paid for each order.

To calculate this value, you will need to check which customer each row in the *DELIVERIES* worksheet refers to, and then look up the delivery charge for that customer on the *CHARGES* worksheet.

To do this, you will use a reference function, VLOOKUP.

VLOOKUP

VLOOKUP is an Excel function that checks a cell range for a row starting with a specified value, and returns the value in a specified column of that row. (The *V* in the function name indicates that the lookup is *Vertical*. That is, the lookup checks a cell range vertically till it finds a row starting with a particular value.)

The reference function VLOOKUP has the following format:

=VLOOKUP(Lookup_value, Table_array, Col_index_num, Range_lookup)	
Lookup_value	The value to look for in the first column of the *Table_array*.
Table_array	The cell range to look at. Entries in the *Table_array* must be sorted by the first column in ascending order if you specify a value of *1* for *Range_lookup*.

=VLOOKUP(Lookup_value, Table_array, Col_index_num, Range_lookup)	
Col_index_num	The number (not letter) for the column in the table array that contains the value you want returned.
Range_lookup	*1* (*TRUE*) or *0* (*FALSE*). If you leave this value blank, 0 is used by default. If *Range_lookup* is *1*, then if the *Lookup_value* is not found, the row starting with the closest value *less than* the *Lookup_value* is used instead. This is why the entries in the *Table_array* must be sorted by the first column in ascending order if this option is used. If *Range_lookup* is *0*, then an error will be given if an exact match to your *Lookup_value* is not found in the first column of the *Table_array*.

Note: The parts of the function in the brackets are called parameters. These values should always separated by commas.

Some parameters are optional, and you do not have to specify a value for them; if you do not supply a value, you should include a blank space instead of that parameter, and separate it from the other parameter values using commas so that Excel knows that the next value given should be used for the parameter *after* the one you are skipping. If an optional parameter comes at the end of the parameter list, you can simply leave it out and not worry about typing the extra commas.

In the next exercise, you will use the VLOOKUP function to find the corresponding *Delivery Charge* in column *C* on the *CHARGES* worksheet for the *CompanyName* in column *B* of every record on the *DELIVERIES* worksheet.

Exercise 11.2: Using VLOOKUP

1. Open DELIVERIES.XLS (or Ex9.3-DELIVERIES.xls) and go to the *DELIVERIES* worksheet.
2. Label column *C Delivery charge*.
3. In cell *C2* on the *DELIVERIES* worksheet, enter the following formula:
   =*VLOOKUP(B2,CHARGES!$A$1:$C$7,3)*
   This formula does the following:
   - Checks the company name listed in cell *B2* of the *DELIVERIES* worksheet
   - Looks at the table array *A1:C7* on the *CHARGES* worksheet
   - Finds a row in the table array that starts with the matching company name
   - Returns the value in the third column of the matched row.
4. Copy the formula to the other cells in column *C*.

Note: The relative *B2* cell reference is updated to reflect the appropriate row in the copied formulae, but the absolute references used to define the table array mean that the same cell range on the *CHARGES* worksheet is used in each formula.

Column *C* now contains the charge for each delivery listed.

Over to you: mandatory

Next, you will work out how much was spent on petrol for each delivery.

- Open DELIVERIES.XLS (or Ex11.2-DELIVERIES.xls).

- Label column *D* on the *DELIVERIES* worksheet *Petrol*.

- In cell *D2* enter a formula that multiplies the distance to the customer listed in cell B2 for each delivery by 2 to get the round-trip distance, and then by £0.06 (the average cost Mr Murphy pays for petrol per km). Use a VLOOKUP function to find the distance to the customer in the same table array used in the last exercise.

- Copy this formula to the other cells in column *D*.

HLOOKUP

A similar function to VLOOKUP, called HLOOKUP, checks a cell range for a column starting with a specified value, and returns the value in a specified row of that column. (The *H* in the function name indicates that the lookup is *Horizontal*. That is, the lookup checks a cell range horizontally till it finds a column starting with a particular value.)

The reference function HLOOKUP has the following format:

=HLOOKUP(Lookup_value, Table_array, Col_index_num, Range_lookup)	
Lookup_value	The value to look for in the first row of the *Table_array*.
Table_array	The cell range to look at. Entries in the *Table_array* must be sorted by the first row in ascending order if you specify a value of *1* for *Range_lookup*.
Row_index_num	The number for the row in the table array that contains the value you want returned.
Range_lookup	*1* (*TRUE*) or *0* (*FALSE*). If you leave this value blank, *0* is used by default. If *Range_lookup* is *1*, then if the *Lookup_value* is not found, the column starting with the closest value *less than* the *Lookup_value* is used instead. This is why the entries in the *Table_array* must be sorted by the first row in ascending order if you want to use this option. If *Range_lookup* is *0*, then an error will be given if an exact match to your *Lookup_value* is not found in the first row of the *Table_array*.

Next, you will work out the delivery charge for each order using a transposed table array and HLOOKUP.

Exercise 11.3: Using HLOOKUP

1. Open DELIVERIES.XLS (or Ex11.2-OTYM1-DELIVERIES.xls), insert a new worksheet and name it *CHARGES2*.
2. Copy the cell range *A1:C7* of the *DELIVERIES* worksheet and use **Paste Special**'s *Transpose* option to paste the values to cell range *A1:G3* of the *CHARGES2* worksheet.
3. In cell *E2* on the *DELIVERIES* worksheet, enter the following formula:
   =HLOOKUP(B2,CHARGES2!$A$1:$G$3,3)
   This formula does the following:
   - Checks the company name listed in cell *B2* of the *DELIVERIES* worksheet
   - Looks at the table array *A1:G3* on the *CHARGES2* worksheet
   - Finds a column in the table array that starts with the matching company name
   - Returns the value in the third row of the matched column.
4. Copy the formula to the other cells in column *E*.
   The values in column E should match those in column C.
5. Save your workbook when you are done.

Subtotalling

Now you know the charge and the cost of petrol for each delivery. Next, you will work out what the monthly total for each one is, using Excel's **Subtotals** command.

The **Subtotals** command allows you to create subtotals of the values in specified columns in a sorted list. Excel looks for changes in the values in specified sorted columns to identify the end of a group, and adds a subtotal at that point.

In the next exercise, you will sort the data on the *DELIVERIES* worksheet of DELIVERIES.XLS by month, and calculate monthly subtotals for delivery charges and petrol.

Before calculating monthly subtotals, you will change the format of the entries in the *DeliveryDate* column to show the month and year only, otherwise each change in the day of the month will be identified as the end of a group, and you will calculate subtotals for each day instead of for each month.

Exercise 11.4: Calculating subtotals

1. Go to the *DELIVERIES* worksheet of DELIVERIES.XLS (or Ex11.3-DELIVERIES.xls) and select column A.
2. Select **Format | Cells....**
   – or –
   Click the **Format Cells** button on the *Formatting* toolbar.
   The *Format Cells* dialog box opens.
3. Click the **Number** tab.
4. In the *Category* area, select *Date*, and in the *Type* area, select *Mar-01*.
   This will format the dates to show only their month and year components.
     Click **OK**.

   Note: Because dates are specified in different ways in different countries, you may not see the *Mar-01* option listed in your default *Date Types*. If this is the case, select the *English (United States)* option from the *Locale* drop-down list below the *Types* area, and the *Mar-01* option should appear.

5. Select columns A to D, and then select **Data | Subtotals....**
   The *Subtotal* dialog box opens.
6. In the *At each change in* field, select *DeliveryDate*.
   In the *Use function* field, select *Sum*.
   In the *Add subtotal to* area, check the boxes beside *Delivery Charge* and *Petrol*
   Your dialog box should now look like this:

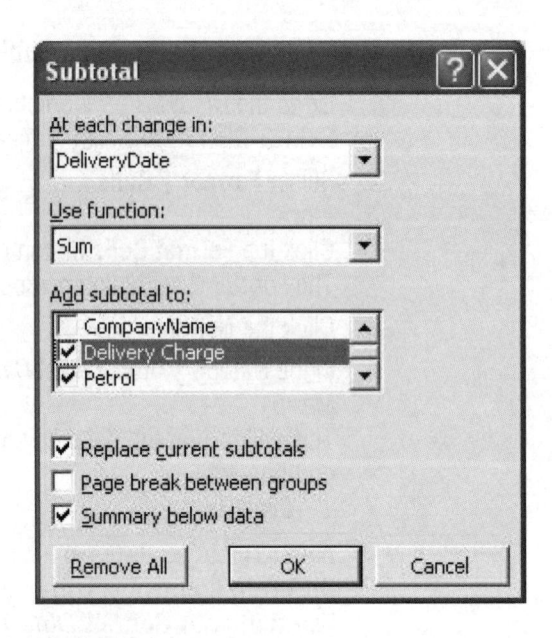

Click **OK**.
Excel calculates subtotals for the specified columns, and adds them to your worksheet.

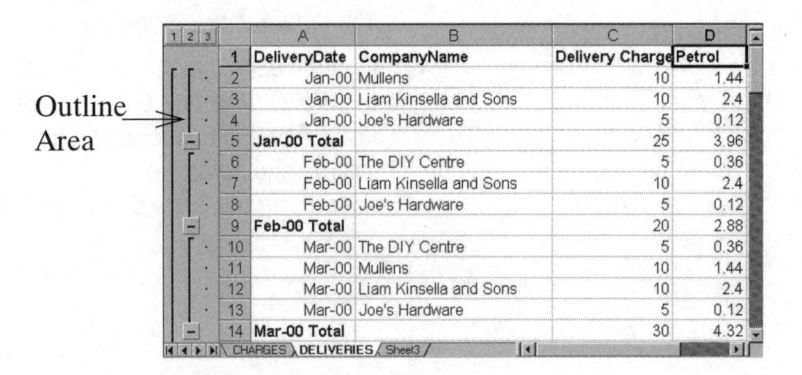

Outline Area

7. Click the '-' symbols in the *Outline* area to hide the record rows, and show only the subtotal results.

8. Save your workbook when you are done.

Over to you: mandatory

Next, you will add the subtotals for each month from DELIVERIES.XLS (or Ex11.4-DELIVERIES.xls) to MFPF_FINANCE.XLS (or Ex11.1-OTYM2-MFPF_FINANCE.xls).

- Using **Copy** and **Paste Special**, copy the monthly revenue from deliveries, and the monthly petrol expenses to the spaces left for them on the *INCOMING* and *OUTGOING* worksheets of MFPF_FINANCE.XLS (or Ex11.1-OTYM2-MFPF_FINANCE.xls). Save both workbooks when you are done, and close DELIVERIES.XLS (or Ex11.4-DELIVERIES.xls).

Note: If you try to select and copy the cell range containing the results, you will also copy the cells in the hidden rows in between the results. You can either copy each subtotal one at a time, or else you can use the **Go To** command to select visible cells in the range only.
To use the **Go To** command: select the cell range containing the subtotal results (the record rows should all be hidden), click **Edit | GoTo...** and on the **Go To** dialog that appears click **Special** to open the **Go To Special** dialog where you can specify that *Visible Cells Only* should be selected. Click **OK** and of the full cell range you originally selected, now only the visible cells are selected.

3D sum

In ECDL 3 or ECDL 4, you learned how to use the SUM function to add up the values in a 2D cell range, that is, values in columns and rows on a single worksheet. You can also use the SUM function to sum in three dimensions, across a series of worksheets, where the numbers you want to add up appear in the same cell or cell range on each worksheet.

A 3D sum function has the following format:

=SUM(First_sheet:Last_sheet!Cell)	
First_sheet	The first worksheet in the 3D range.
Last_sheet	The last worksheet in the 3D range.
Cell	The cell or cell range on all of the worksheets in the specified range that contains the values you want to sum.

On the *INCOMING* and *OUTGOING* worksheets of MFPF_FINANCE.XLS (or Ex11.4-OTYM1-MFPF_FINANCE.xls), the total amounts of money each year that are earned by the business and paid out by the business are calculated in cell *C15*.

In the next exercise, you will add a 3D sum to the *PROFIT* worksheet, which adds up the values that appear in cell *C15* on each sheet.

Exercise 11.5: Creating a 3D sum

1. Go to the *PROFIT* worksheet of MFPF_FINANCE.XLS (or Ex11.4-OTYM1-MFPF_FINANCE.xls).
2. Select cell *C15*.
3. Click the **Autosum** button on the *Standard* toolbar.
4. Go to the *INCOMING* worksheet and select cell *C15*.
5. Hold down the **Shift** key and click the tab for the *OUTGOING* worksheet.
6. Press **Enter**.
7. Save your workbook when you are done.

Autosum button

Σ

The total calculated by adding together the values in cell *C15* on each of the worksheets is now displayed in cell *C15* on the *PROFIT* worksheet.

> **Note:** The result of the calculation does not have to appear in the same cell or cell range as the data used in the sum – it's just a coincidence that in this case it does. However, the data used in the sum *does* have to appear in the same cell or cell range on each of the sheets in the 3D range for this formula to work. If your data appears in different cells on each worksheet, you can use a simple addition formula to add the values together instead.

SUMIF

You can specify that you want to sum data only if they satisfy certain criteria, using Excel's SUMIF function.

The mathematical function SUMIF has the following format:

=SUMIF(Range_to_eval, Criteria, Sum_range)	
Range_to_eval	The range of cells to check against your criteria.
Criteria	The tests to perform to see whether or not to include the data in the sum.
Sum_range	The range of cells containing the data you want to sum. If you do not specify an alternative *Sum_range*, the values in the *Range_to_eval* will be summed. There should be a 1-to-1 correspondence between cells in the *Range_to_eval* and *Sum_range*.

Note: Criteria are enclosed in quotation marks and can be any comparisons using the expressions <, >, =, <= (which means less than or equal to) or >= (which means greater than or equal to), and can include cell references as well as numeric and text values.

MFPF currently require a minimum order of 8 for garden chairs. Mr Murphy is thinking about increasing this number to 12. He has asked you to look at last year's figures and work out how many chairs would have been sold if MFPF had refused to fill orders for under 12 chairs at a time.

In the next exercise, you will calculate how many chairs were sold last year in total, and how many of them were sold in orders for 12 or more chairs.

Exercise 11.6: Using the SUMIF function

1. Open MFPF_ORD.XLS (or Ex10.2-MFPF_ORD.xls) and go to the *COMPLETE* worksheet.
2. In cell *I56*, below the column giving order numbers for garden chairs, enter the formula =*SUM(I2:I55)*.
3. In cell *I57* enter the formula =*SUMIF(I2:I55, ">=12")*.

ECDL Advanced Spreadsheets for Microsoft® Office XP and 2003

The number in cell *I57* is smaller than the number in *I56*, because only those orders for 12 or more chairs were included in the sum.

Over to you: optional

Next, check how many garden tables would have been sold if no order for under three tables at a time was filled. Save and close the workbook when you are done.

SUMPOSITIVE

As you may know, ECDL is a vendor-independent certification. One of the Advanced Spreadsheets syllabus requirements is to know about SUMPOSITIVE. SUMPOSITIVE is a Lotus 1-2-3 function that sums only the positive values in a cell range. You can use Excel's SUMIF function to create the equivalent formula
=SUMIF(Range_to_eval, ">0", Sum_range).

ROUND

Occasionally you will want to round numbers on a spreadsheet to a particular number of decimal places. Excel's ROUND function allows you to specify any number of digits before or after the decimal point to which you can round the number.

The mathematical function ROUND has the following format:

=ROUND(Number, Num_digits)	
Number	The number you want to round.
Num_digits	The number of digits before or after the decimal point to round to. A negative number indicates a position to the left of the decimal point, and a positive number indicates a position to the right.

Mrs Murphy has asked you to provide her with a list of the monthly profits on the *PROFIT* worksheet of MFPF_FINANCE.XLS (or Ex11.5-MFPF_FINANCE.xls), with each value rounded to the nearest £100.

In the next exercise, you will add a column to the *PROFIT* worksheet which shows rounded profit figures for each month.

Exercise 11.7: Using the ROUND function

1. Open MFPF_FINANCE.XLS (or Ex11.5-MFPF_FINANCE.xls) and go to the *PROFIT* worksheet.
2. Label column E *Rounded Profit*.
3. In cell *E2* enter the formula =*ROUND(D2, –2)*.
4. Copy the formula to the cells *E3:E13*.
   Column E now shows the profits for each month of the year rounded to the nearest £100.

D	E
Profit	Rounded Profit
3482.84	3500
1057.70	1100
605.32	600
465.94	500
3060.26	3100
2590.76	2600
3695.02	3700
2997.06	3000
508.74	500
185.98	200
1648.84	1600
598	600

Nesting

In the previous exercise, you used the ROUND function to manipulate a number generated by a SUM function. You could have combined both functions in a single formula by nesting them.

If you use one function as an argument in another function, then the first function is nested in the second. Nested functions should be placed within round brackets, called parentheses '( )'.

You can nest up to seven functions inside a function.

In the next exercise you will create a nested function to calculate the profit figure for a month, *and* round it to the nearest £100.

Exercise 11.8: Nesting functions

1. Open MFPF_FINANCE.XLS (or Ex11.7-MFPF_FINANCE.xls) and go to the *PROFIT* worksheet.
2. Label column F *Rounded Profit (using nesting)*.
3. In cell *F2* enter =*ROUND(SUM(B2:C2),–2)*.
   This formula first calculates the sum of the values in the cells in the cell range *B2:C2*, and then applies the ROUND function to show the result rounded to the nearest hundreds value.
4. Copy the formula to cells *F3:F13*.

The results in column F are identical to those in column E and were achieved using just one formula.

When you are done, save and close your workbook.

Chapter summary

VLOOKUP is an Excel function that checks a cell range vertically for a row starting with a specified value, and returns the value in a specified column of that row.

HLOOKUP is an Excel function that checks a cell range horizontally for a column starting with a specified value, and returns the value in a specified row of that column.

The **Subtotals** command allows you to create subtotals of values in a sorted list. Excel looks for changes in the values in one specified column to identify the end of a group, and creates a subtotal at that point.

You can use the SUM function to sum in three dimensions, across a series of worksheets, where the numbers you want to add up appear in the same cell or cell range on each worksheet.

You can specify that you want to include data in a calculation only if they satisfy certain criteria, using the SUMIF function.

The ROUND function allows you to specify any number of digits before or after the decimal point to which the number is to be rounded.

You can combine a number of functions in a single formula by nesting them inside one another, using parentheses.

Quick Quiz

Circle the answer to each of the following multiple-choice questions about reference and mathematical functions in Excel.

Q1	VLOOKUP and HLOOKUP functions import data they look up in external databases.
A.	True.
B.	False.

Q2	Which of the following HLOOKUP(Lookup_value, Table_array, Col_index_num, Range_lookup) parameters is optional?
A.	Range_lookup
B.	Table_array
C.	Col_index_num
D.	Lookup_value

Q3	The results of a 3D SUM function must appear in the same cell or cell range on the final worksheet as the source data on the other worksheets.
A.	True.
B.	False.

Q4	How many functions can you nest inside another?
A.	3
B.	7
C.	9
D.	As many as you like.

ECDL Advanced Spreadsheets for Microsoft® Office XP and 2003

Q5	Nested functions should be placed in:
A.	Square brackets '[ ]'.
B	Round brackets '( )'.
C.	Curly brackets '{ }'.
D.	Quotation marks.

Answers

1: B; **2:** A; **3:** B; **4:** B; **5:** B.

Chapter 12: Customising charts

In this chapter

In ECDL 3 or ECDL 4, you learned how to create charts in Excel, and how to make simple changes to them.

In this chapter you will learn how to make more advanced changes to Excel charts.

New skills

At the end of this chapter you should be able to:

- Delete a data series from a chart
- Change the angle of pie chart slices
- Explode all the segments in a pie chart
- Format the text or numbers on a chart axis
- Reposition chart titles, legends and data labels
- Widen the gap between columns or bars in a chart
- Insert an image into a chart

New words

There are no new words in this chapter.

Syllabus reference

The following syllabus items are covered in this chapter:

- AM 4.2.5.1 – Change angle of pie chart slices.
- AM 4.2.5.2 – Format chart axes numbers or text.
- AM 4.2.5.3 – Re-position title, legend, or data labels in a chart.
- AM 4.2.5.4 – 'Explode' all the segments in a pie chart.
- AM 4.2.5.5 – Delete a data series in a chart.
- AM 4.2.5.6 – Modify the chart type for a defined data series.
- AM 4.2.5.7 – Widen the gap between columns / bars in a 2D chart.
- AM 4.2.5.8 – Insert an image in a 2D chart.

Deleting a data series from a chart

A data series is a set of related data in an Excel chart and items belonging to a particular data series share a common colour or pattern. A single chart may contain a number of data series.

Sometimes you may find that after you have created a chart, you need to remove a particular data series. Maybe one data series dominates the chart, making it difficult to see the others. Maybe you accidentally included values for a salesperson who deals with a different geographical area from the one covered by the chart.

You could delete your chart, reselect the source data, and generate a new chart which shows only the relevant data series.

But Excel allows you to edit the chart directly and remove the data series there, preserving any other changes you have made in the meantime.

> **Note:** You can also *add* data series to a chart after it has been created. To do this, you should select the extra data series (including corresponding labels, if appropriate) on the relevant worksheet, copy the data, then select your chart and paste the copied data. Being able to add extra data series to a chart is not a requirement of the ECDL Advanced Spreadsheets syllabus, so is not covered in any more detail here.

Mrs Murphy has asked you to generate a chart that shows the sales of each product each month over the year.

In the next exercise, you will create the chart, and add it to a new worksheet in MFPF_FINANCE.XLS (or Ex11.8-MFPF_FINANCE.xls).

Exercise 12.1: Creating a column chart

1. Open MFPF_FINANCE.XLS (or Ex11.8-MFPF_FINANCE.xls) and select the named cell range *SALES*.
2. Select **Insert | Chart...**.
   – or –

Chart Wizard button

Click the **Chart Wizard** button on the *Standard* toolbar.
The *Chart Wizard* dialog box appears.

3. In the *Type* area, select *Column*.
   In the *Subtype* area, select *Clustered Column with a 3D visual effect*.

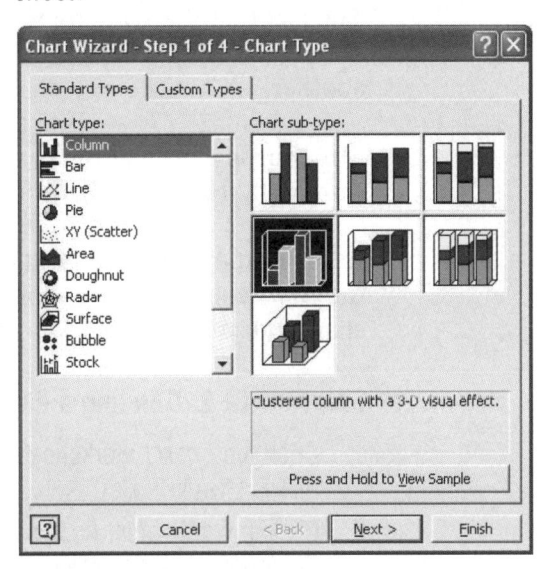

4. Click **Next** until you get to the last screen in the *Chart Wizard*: *Chart Location*.

5. Select *Add as new sheet*, and click **Finish**.
   Your chart is created and added to a new worksheet named *Chart1*.
   Your chart should look like this:

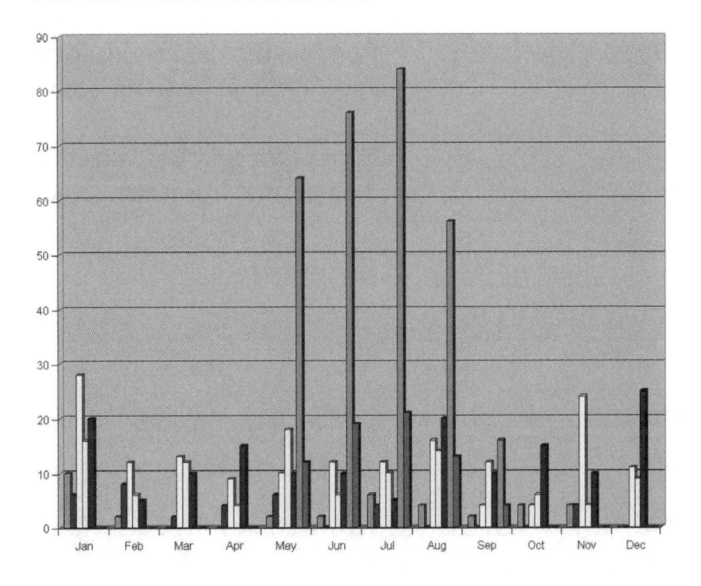

There is a trend for a *lot* of garden furniture to be bought in the summer months. Because of these high summer sales, the data series for garden chairs swamps the rest of the data in the chart.

The fact that there are up to seven columns in each cluster also makes it difficult to distinguish one column from another.

Mrs Murphy looks at the chart, and asks you to change it to show data for sales of bedroom furniture only.

In the next exercise, you will begin to delete data series from the chart you already generated, instead of regenerating the chart with the required data only.

Exercise 12.2: Deleting a data series from a chart

1. Open the *Chart1* worksheet of MFPF_FINANCE.XLS (or Ex12.1-MFPF_FINANCE.xls).
2. Click any data point (in this case, any column) in the *Garden Chair* data series to select the whole data series, and press the **Delete** key.
   – or –
   Right-click any data point in the *Garden Chair* data series and select **Clear** from the shortcut menu that appears.
   The data series is deleted from the chart.

Over to you: mandatory

Remove the data series for *Garden Table*, *Kitchen Organizer* and *Coffee Table* in the same way.

Your chart now contains three columns in each cluster of data points. It is much easier to read than the original graph.

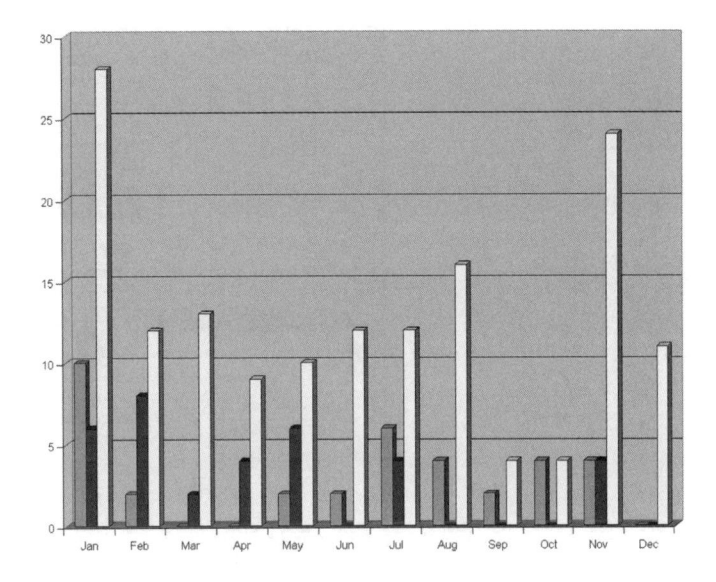

Save the workbook when you are done.

Modifying the chart type for a data series

MFPF have a black and white printer and the Murphys are worried that the distinction between each of the data series in the chart may not be as clear on paper as it is on the screen. Luckily, Excel allows you to represent each data series in a chart in a different chart type which will make it much clearer which one is which. You decide to apply a different chart type to each data series in your chart to improve the chart's readability.

In the next exercise, you will change the chart type for the *Wardrobe* data series to *Cylinder*.

Exercise 12.3: Changing the chart type for a data series

1. Open the *Chart1* worksheet of MFPF_FINANCE.XLS (or Ex12.2-MFPF_FINANCE.xls).
2. Right-click the *Wardrobe* data series, and select **Chart Type** from the shortcut menu that opens.
   The *Chart Type* dialog box appears.
3. In the *Chart Type* area, select *Cylinder*.
4. In the *Options* area, select *Apply to selection* to change the chart type for the selected data series only.

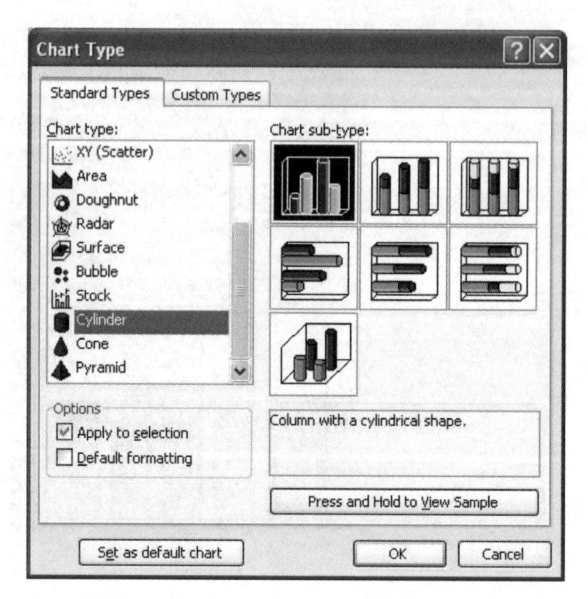

5. Click **OK**.

Over to you: mandatory

Next, change the chart type for the *Chest of Drawers* data series to *Cone* on the *Chart1* worksheet of MFPF_FINANCE.XLS (or Ex12.3-MFPF_FINANCE.xls).

Save the workbook when you are done.

Formatting chart axes

You can change the font attributes for any text that appears in your chart.

You decide to make some more changes to the chart to improve the legibility of the data shown.

In the next exercise, you will change the font attributes of the text on the axes of the chart.

Exercise 12.4: Formatting chart axes

1. Open the *Chart1* worksheet of MFPF_FINANCE.XLS (or Ex12.3-OTYM1-MFPF_FINANCE.xls).
2. Right-click the horizontal axis showing the months of the year to select it.
   A small square appears at each end of the axis line when it is selected.

3. Select **Format Axis** from the shortcut menu that appears.
   The *Format Axis* dialog box opens.
4. Click the **Font** tab.
5. Assign the following font settings:
   - *Font*: *Verdana*
   - *Size*: *11*
   - *Color*: *Dark blue*
6. Click **OK**.
   Your font format changes are applied to the text on the axis.

Over to you: mandatory

On the *Chart1* worksheet of MFPF_FINANCE.XLS (or Ex12.4-MFPF_FINANCE.xls), format the numbers on the vertical axis to appear with the same font settings as the labels on the horizontal axis.

Widening the gaps between columns in a chart

Excel adds a certain amount of space between the columns in a chart by default. You can change how much space appears between columns if you want.

Mrs Murphy asks you to change your chart to a 2D column representation, and to add extra space between the column clusters and between the columns in each cluster to see what effect that has on the chart's readability.

In the next exercise, you will change the chart type for all the data series, and add extra space between the columns in each cluster and between the individual clusters.

Exercise 12.5: Widening the gaps between columns in a 2D chart

1. Open the *Chart1* worksheet of MFPF_FINANCE.XLS (or Ex12.4-OTYM1-MFPF_FINANCE.xls).
2. Right-click any data series in your chart, and select **Chart Type** from the shortcut menu that opens.
   The *Chart Type* dialog box appears.
3. In the *Chart Type* area, select *Column*.
4. Make sure that the check box beside *Apply to selection* is *unchecked*.

5. Click **OK**.
   The chart is reformatted so that all data series are 2D columns.
6. Right-click any data point in any data series, and select **Format Data Series** from the shortcut menu that opens.
   The *Format Data Series* dialog box opens.
7. Click the **Options** tab.

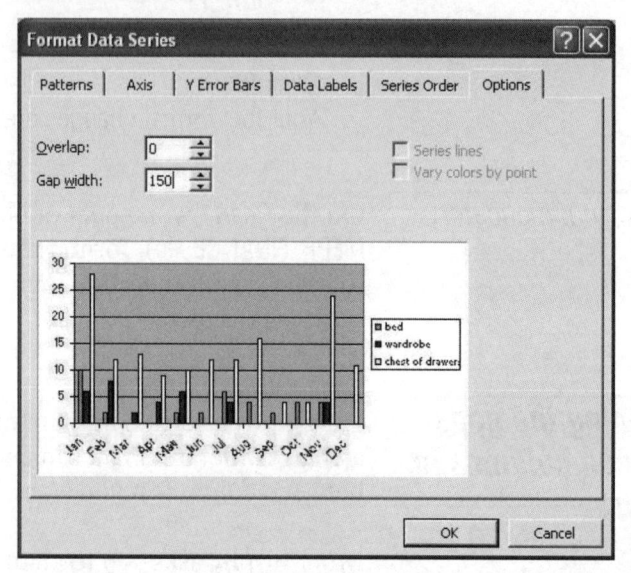

8. In the *Overlap* field, enter *–50*, either by entering the number in the box, or by using the up/down arrows to the right of the box to change the value.
   Overlap refers to the size of the gap between the columns in each cluster.
   In the *Gap width* field, enter *400*.
   Gap width refers to the gap between adjacent clusters.
   The graph on the lower half of the tab changes to show the effect of your changes.
9. Click **OK**.
   Extra space is added between the columns in each cluster and between each of the clusters too.

Inserting a picture in a chart

Excel allows you to add a graphic to the plot area, the chart area, a data series, or a data point in your chart.

You decide to change the default background of the plot area to the MFPF logo.

In the next exercise, you will add the company logo as a background to the chart area.

Exercise 12.6: Adding a graphic to a chart

1. Open the *Chart1* worksheet of MFPF_FINANCE.XLS (or Ex12.5-MFPF_FINANCE.xls).
2. Right-click the plot area and select *Format Plot Area* from the shortcut menu that opens.
   The *Format Plot Area* dialog box opens.

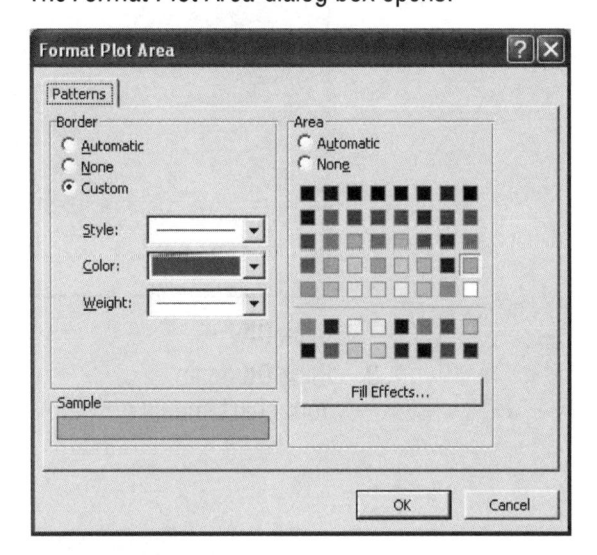

3. Click **Fill Effects...**.
   The *Fill Effects* dialog box opens.
4. Click the **Picture** tab.
5. Click **Select Picture...**.
   The *Select Picture* dialog box opens.
6. Select the file LOGO.GIF from your working folder, and click **Insert**.

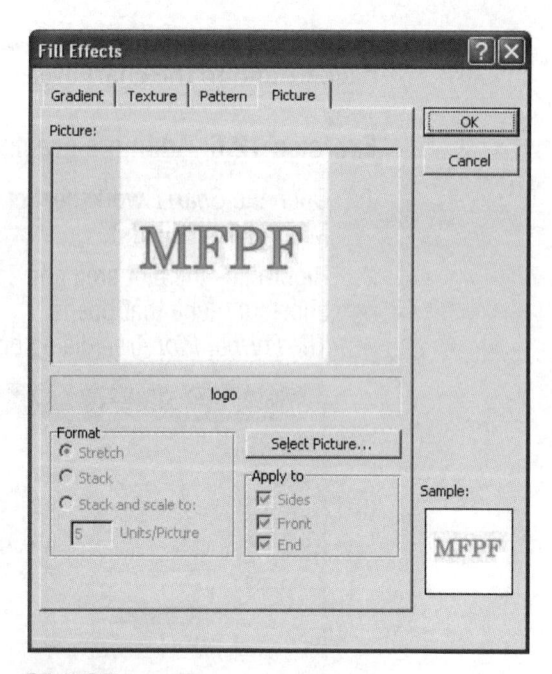

7. Click **OK**.
8. Click **OK** again.
   Your chart should now look like this:

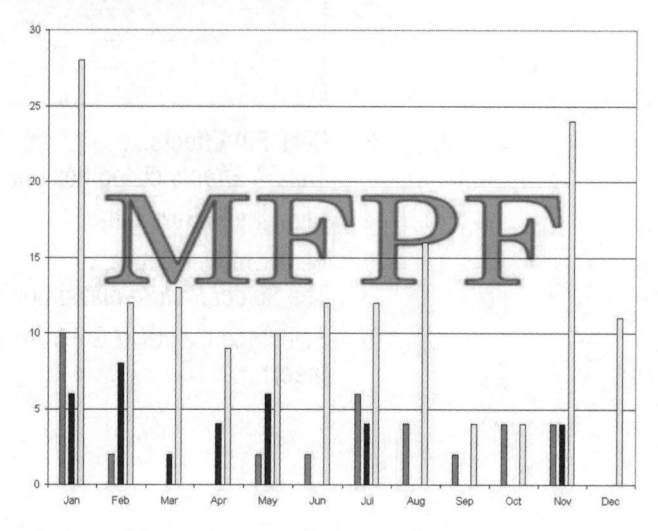

Save your workbook when you are done.

Changing the angle of slices in a pie chart

When you insert a pie chart, the order of the slices is determined by the order of the values in the worksheet cells used to generate the chart. While you cannot change the order the slices appear in in the chart, you *can* rotate a pie chart to change the angle at which the first slice appears relative to the 12 o'clock position.

July was the busiest month for MFPF. Mrs Murphy has asked you to generate a pie chart showing the breakdown of sales in that month.

In the next exercise you will generate a pie chart showing the sales of each furniture type for the month of July.

Exercise 12.7: Creating a pie chart

1. Go to the *SALES TOTALS* worksheet of MFPF_FINANCE.XLS (or Ex12.6-MFPF_FINANCE.xls).
2. Select the non-adjacent cell ranges *A1:H1* and *A8:H8*.
3. Select **Insert | Chart....**
   – or –
   Click the **Chart Wizard** button on the *Standard* toolbar.
   The *Chart Wizard* opens.
4. In the *Type* area, select *Pie*.
5. Click **Next** until you get to the last screen in the *Chart Wizard*: *Chart Location*.
6. Select *Add as new sheet*, and click **Finish**.
   Your chart is created and added to a new worksheet named *Chart2*.

Garden chairs make up most of the sales. Mrs Murphy would like the pie slice representing garden chairs to be the last one in the pie, ending at the 12 o'clock position.

In the next exercise, you will change the angle of the pie chart, so that the pie slice for garden chairs appears last. You will also add data labels to each slice to show how many units of furniture each one represents.

Exercise 12.8: Changing the angle of slices in a pie chart

1. Go to the *Chart2* worksheet of MFPF_FINANCE.XLS (or Ex12.7-MFPF_FINANCE.xls).
2. Right-click the pie chart and select *Format Data Series* from the shortcut menu that opens.
   The *Format Data Series* dialog box opens.

3. Click the **Options** tab.

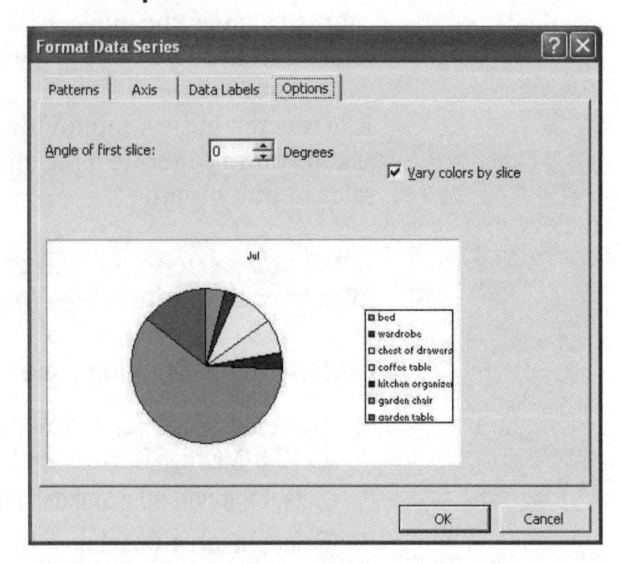

4. Change the value in the *Angle of first slice* box, either by entering the number in the box, or by using the up/down arrows to the right of the box to change the value.
   If you use the up/down arrows to change the angle, you can see the pie chart rotate in the preview area on this screen.
   In this case, the angle of the first slice should be 54 degrees.

5. Click the **Data Labels** tab.

6. In the *Data labels* area, select *Show values*. (In Excel 2003, select *Values* in the *Label contains* area.)

7. Click **OK**.
   Your pie chart is rotated as specified on the Options tab, and data labels have been added to each slice, showing the number of units of each furniture type sold.

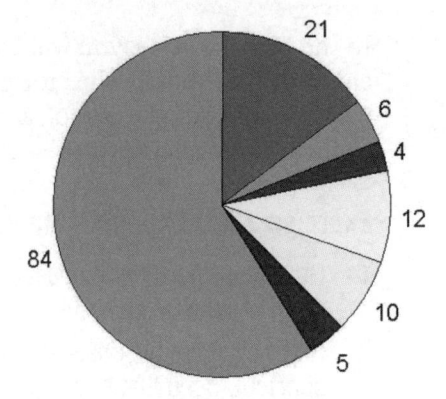

Exploding all the slices in a pie chart

In ECDL 3 or ECDL 4 you learned how to explode individual slices in a pie to make them easier to see. There is also a pie chart subtype called *Exploded Pie*, in which all of the slices of the pie chart are exploded.

It is easier to change the chart subtype than to explode each slice individually.

In the next exercise, you will change the chart subtype from *Pie* to *Exploded Pie*, so that you can see the smaller slices more clearly.

Exercise 12.9: Changing the chart type

1. Go to the *Chart2* worksheet of MFPF_FINANCE.XLS (or Ex12.8-MFPF_FINANCE.xls).
2. Right-click the pie chart, and select **Chart Type** from the shortcut menu that opens.
   The *Chart Type* dialog box appears.
3. *Pie* is already selected in the *Type* area.
   In the *Subtype* area, select *Exploded pie*.
4. Click **OK**.
   Your chart is now an exploded pie chart.

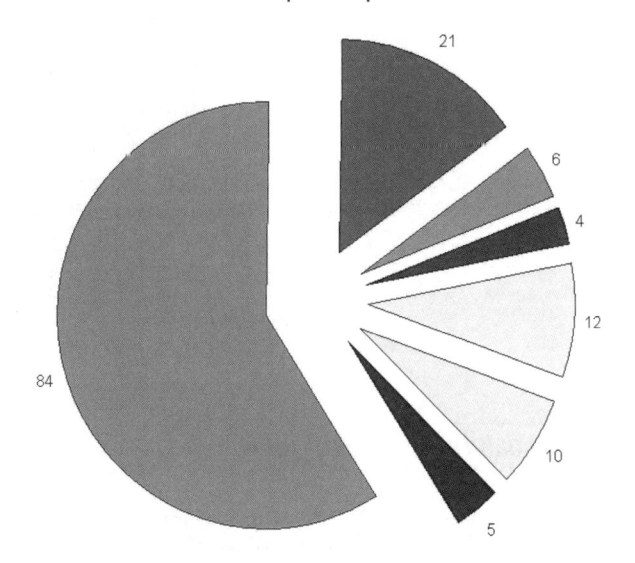

Repositioning chart elements

The chart title, legend and data labels are added to default positions in a chart in Excel. If you would prefer to see them in different positions, you can select any one of them and drag it to any other position on the chart that you like.

In the next exercise, you will reposition the title of the pie chart, so that instead of appearing above the chart, it appears just to the left of it.

Exercise 12.10: Repositioning a chart title

1. Go to the *Chart2* worksheet of MFPF_FINANCE.XLS (or Ex12.9-MFPF_FINANCE.xls).
2. Select the chart title, *Jul*, by clicking it once.
   A rectangle of small black boxes appears around the text box when it is selected.
3. Click the border of the text box, and drag it to its new position, just left of the chart.

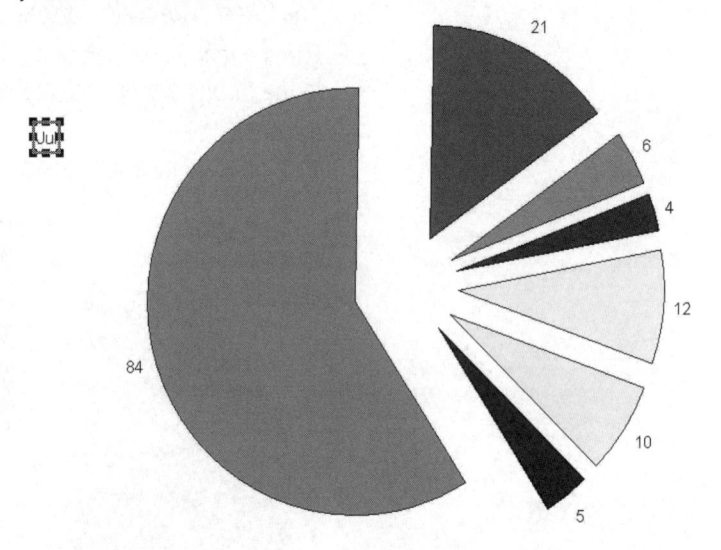

Over to you: mandatory

Next, you will move some other chart elements.

- Go to the *Chart2* worksheet of MFPF_FINANCE.XLS (or Ex12.10-MFPF_FINANCE.xls).

- Move the legend, by default located in a box to the right of the chart, to just below the chart title on the left of the chart.
- Drag the data labels for each pie slice onto the relevant slice.

When you are done, save and close MFPF_FINANCE.XLS.

Chapter summary

You can make changes to a chart after it has been created. You can remove individual data series, or represent each data series in a chart by a different chart type.

You can change the font attributes for any text in your chart.

You can change how much space appears between columns in a column chart, or rotate a pie chart to change the angle at which the first slice appears relative to the 12 o'clock position.

You can add graphics to the plot area, the chart area, data series, and data points in your chart.

You can move chart elements to new positions if you are not happy with the default layout.

Quick Quiz

Circle the answer to each of the following multiple-choice questions about customising Excel charts.

Q1	To add or delete data series in a chart, you must recreate the chart entirely.
A.	True.
B.	False.

Q2	Each data series in a chart can be shown in a different chart type.
A.	True.
B.	False.

Q3	To widen the gaps between columns in a chart, you should:
A.	Click and drag the columns to their new positions.
B.	Use the **Format Data Series** option to specify *Overlap* and *Gap*.
C.	Select a chart type with bigger gaps.
D.	Add blank cells between the data series values in your data source.

Q4	If you don't like the orientation of the slices in a pie chart you should...
A.	Change the order of the data series values in the source data.
B.	Drag and drop the slices to new positions.
C.	Label the data series you want to appear at the 12 o'clock position with the label 'First'.
D.	Rotate the pie chart.

Q5	To add a background image to a chart, you associate it with the...
A.	Chart type.
B.	Plot area.
C.	Data series.
D.	Worksheet.

Answers **1:** B; **2:** A; **3:** B; **4:** D; **5:** B.

Chapter 13: Using statistical and database functions

In this chapter

Sometimes, you will want to count the number of cells in a range that contain a particular type of data, although you don't want to do anything with the values in the cells.

In this chapter, you will learn how to count the number of cells in a range that contains a certain type of value, or that satisfy specified criteria.

You will also learn about Excel 'databases', and find out how to count fields and sum the values they contain using criteria to specify which fields to include. You will also learn how to find minimum and maximum values in Excel database fields.

New skills

At the end of this chapter you should be able to:

- Use the COUNT function
- Use the COUNTA function
- Use the COUNTIF function
- Use the DSUM function
- Use the DMIN and DMAX functions
- Use the DCOUNT function

New words

At the end of this chapter you should be able to explain the following term:

- Excel database

Syllabus reference

The following syllabus items are covered in this chapter:

- AM 4.3.1.3 – Use statistical functions: COUNT; PURECOUNT; COUNTA; COUNTIF.
- AM 4.3.1.8 – Use available database functions: DSUM; DMIN; DMAX and DCOUNT.

Statistical functions

The statistical functions you will learn about in this chapter are used to count the number of cells in a cell range that contain a particular type of data, or data that satisfy specified criteria.

COUNT

COUNT is an Excel function that looks at a list of values and calculates how many of them are numeric. Blanks and text values are disregarded.

The statistical function COUNT has the following format:

COUNT(Value1, Value2, ...)	
Value1, Value2, ...	A list of values or a cell range containing the data elements to count. Only the numeric values are counted.

Mr Murphy asks you to calculate exactly how many orders were made in the year.

You could calculate the total number of orders by looking at the row number of the first entry and the row number of the last, and subtracting one from the other. But using COUNT, you can simply tell Excel to look at any of the columns which contain order numbers, and count how many entries in that range are numbers.

In the next exercise, you will use COUNT to calculate how many of the cells in column J contain numeric values and thereby determine how many orders were made.

> **Note:** If you completed the optional SUMIF exercise on page 130, you should delete the SUM and SUMIF formulae you added in column J of the *COMPLETE* worksheet in MFPF_ORD.XLS (or Ex11.6-MFPF_ORD.xls). The results of these formulae are numeric values, and will be counted by the functions in the following exercises.

Exercise 13.1: Using COUNT

1. Open MFPF_ORD.XLS (or Ex11.6-MFPF_ORD.xls) and go to the *COMPLETE* worksheet.
2. In cell *N2*, enter the formula =*COUNT(J:J)* to count all the rows in column J that contain a number.
    The answer is 54.
    Cell *J1*, which contains label text, and the blank cells in the column were not counted.
3. Save your workbook when you are done.

COUNTA

COUNTA is an Excel function that looks at a list of values and counts how many of them are non-blank. Any numeric or textual value will add to the count total.

COUNTA is the Excel function equivalent to Lotus 1-2-3's PURECOUNT.

The statistical function COUNTA has the following format:

COUNTA(Value1, Value2, ...)	
Value1, Value2, ...	A list of values or a cell range containing the data elements to count. All non-blank values are counted.

In the next exercise, you will count how many cells in column J of the *COMPLETE* worksheet of MFPF_ORD.XLS contain values.

Exercise 13.2: Using COUNTA

1. Go to the *COMPLETE* worksheet of MFPF_ORD.XLS (or Ex13.1-MFPF_ORD.xls).
2. In cell *N3*, enter the formula =*COUNTA(J:J)*.
    The answer is 55.
    Cell *J1* contains text, so was included in the count, but the blank cells in the column were ignored again.
3. Save your workbook when you are done.

COUNTIF

COUNTIF is an Excel function that looks at a list of values, and calculates how many of them satisfy specified criteria.

The statistical function COUNTIF has the following format:

COUNTIF(Range, Criteria)	
Range	The cell range containing the values to be counted.
Criteria	The criteria the value in a cell must satisfy for that cell to be included in the count.

Earlier you used SUMIF to see how many chairs MFPF would have sold if no orders for fewer than 12 at a time had been filled. How many actual orders would not have been filled?

In the next exercise, you will use COUNTIF to find the number of values in the *Chairs* column on the *COMPLETE* worksheet of MFPF_ORD.XLS that are lower than 12.

Exercise 13.3: Using COUNTIF

1. Open MFPF_ORD.XLS (or Ex13.2-MFPF_ORD.xls) and go to the *COMPLETE* worksheet.
2. In cell *I58*, enter the formula *=COUNTIF(I2:I55,"<12")*.
   There were 38 in which fewer than 12 chairs were ordered.
3. Save your workbook when you are done.

Database functions

The 'database' referred to in the term 'database function' is not an external one, such as Microsoft Access. It is a table or list of related data in an Excel spreadsheet.

Excel database
An Excel database is a table or list of related data in an Excel spreadsheet that can be treated as a database of records.

Excel database functions are used to make calculations based on the data in specific fields of a table or list row, where the row satisfies specified criteria.

DSUM

DSUM is an Excel function that looks at a list or table of values, finds the rows that satisfy specified criteria, and adds up the values in a specified column of those rows.

The database function DSUM has the following format:

=DSUM(Database, Field, Criteria)	
Database	The cell range you will use as your database for the purposes of this calculation.
Field	The number (not letter) of the column relative to the database cell range that contains the values you want to sum. That is, if the database cell range starts in column D, then column D is numbered 1.
Criteria	The criteria that must be satisfied for the row values to be included in the sum. Criteria for database functions are specified as a range of cell pairs, where one cell contains a column name and the cell below it contains the value that should appear in that column. Each of the criteria specified must be satisfied for the row values to be included in the sum.

In the next exercise, you will use the DSUM function to calculate the total number of garden chairs ordered by the Cullenstown Garden Centre, using the data on the *COMPLETE* worksheet of MFPF_ORD.XLS (or Ex13.3-MFPF_ORD.xls) as your database.

The cell range containing the query results you will use as your database was automatically given the custom name of MFPF_Q1 when you imported the data. You will use that name to identify the cell range in the function.

Note: Although the values in the cell range you will use were imported from a database, that is not a requirement for data in Excel databases – they could equally have been entered by hand.

Exercise 13.4: Using DSUM

1. Go to the *COMPLETE* worksheet of MFPF_ORD.XLS (or Ex13.3-MFPF_ORD.xls).
2. Enter the label *CompanyName* (with no spaces) in cell *N6*. Enter the value *Cullenstown Garden Centre* in cell *N7*.
   This is the criterion you will use to find the rows in the database to include in the sum.
3. In cell *N9*, enter the label *Chairs ordered*.
4. In cell *O9*, enter the formula *=DSUM(MFPF_Q1,9,N6:N7)*.
   This checks the *MFPF_Q1* cell range for rows where the column labelled *CompanyName* has the value *Cullenstown Garden Centre* and sums the values in the ninth column (*Chairs*) of each matching row.
   The result is that 108 chairs were ordered in the year by the Cullenstown Garden Centre.

DMIN

DMIN is an Excel function that looks at a list or table of values, finds the rows that satisfy specified criteria, and determines the minimum value in a specified column of those rows.

The database function DMIN has the following format:

=DMIN(Database, Field, Criteria)	
Database	The cell range you will use as your database for the purposes of this calculation.
Field	The number (not letter) of the column relative to the database cell range in which you want to find a minimum value. That is, if the database cell range starts in column D, then column D is numbered 1.
Criteria	The cell range containing the criteria for the rows to include.

In the next exercise, you will use the DMIN function to find the smallest order for garden chairs placed by the Cullenstown Garden Centre.

Exercise 13.5: Using DMIN

1. Open MFPF_ORD.XLS (or Ex13.4-MFPF_ORD.xls), and go to the *COMPLETE* worksheet.
2. In cell *N10*, enter the label *Smallest chair order*.
3. In cell *O10*, enter the formula *=DMIN(MFPF_Q1,9,N6:N7)*.
   This checks the *MFPF_Q1* cell range for rows where the column labelled *CompanyName* has the value *Cullenstown Garden Centre* and finds the smallest value in the ninth column (*Chairs*) across all matching rows.
   The smallest chair order from Cullenstown Garden Centre was for 8 chairs.

DMAX

DMAX is an Excel function that looks at a list or table of values, finds the rows that satisfy specified criteria, and determines the maximum value in a specified column of those rows.

The database function DMAX has the following format:

=DMAX(Database, Field, Criteria)	
Database	The cell range you will use as your database for the purposes of this calculation.
Field	The number (not letter) of the column relative to the database cell range in which you want to find a maximum value. That is, if the database cell range starts in column D, then column D is numbered 1.
Criteria	The cell range containing the criteria for the rows to include.

In the next exercise, you will use the DMAX function to find the largest order for garden chairs placed by the Cullenstown Garden Centre.

Exercise 13.6: Using DMAX

1. Open MFPF_ORD.XLS (or Ex13.5-MFPF_ORD.xls), and go to the *COMPLETE* worksheet.
2. In cell *N11*, enter the label *Largest chair order*.
3. In cell *O11*, enter the formula *=DMAX(MFPF_Q1,9,N6:N7)*. This checks the *MFPF_Q1* cell range for rows where the column labelled *CompanyName* has the value *Cullenstown Garden Centre* and finds the largest value in the ninth column (*Chairs*) across all matching rows.
   The largest chair order from Cullenstown Garden Centre was for 32 chairs.

DCOUNT

DCOUNT is an Excel function that looks at a list or table of values, finds the rows that satisfy specified criteria, and counts them.

The database function DCOUNT has the following format:

=DCOUNT(Database, Field, Criteria)	
Database	The cell range you will use as your database for the purposes of this calculation.
Field	The number (not letter) of the column relative to the database cell range that contains the values you want to count. That is, if the database cell range starts in column D, then column D is numbered 1.
Criteria	The cell range containing the criteria for the rows to include.

In the next exercise, you will use the DCOUNT function to find how many orders satisfy the following two criteria:

- 12 or more garden chairs were ordered.

and

- The orders were placed by the Cullenstown Garden Centre.

Exercise 13.7: Using DCOUNT

1. Open MFPF_ORD.XLS (or Ex13.6-MFPF_ORD.xls), and go to the *COMPLETE* worksheet.

2. In cell *O6*, enter the criterion label *Chair*.
   In cell *O7*, enter >=12.
3. In cell *N13*, enter the label *12+ chairs*.
4. In cell *O13*, enter the formula =*DCOUNT(MFPF_Q1,9, N6:O7)*.
   This formula tells Excel to count the entries in the ninth column of the *MFPF_Q1* database (named cell range) that match the two criteria defined in the cell range *N6:O7*.
   The result shows that Cullenstown Garden Centre made 6 orders for 12 or more chairs.

Chapter summary

Excel's COUNT function looks at a list of values, and calculates how many of them are numeric. Blanks and text values are disregarded.

The COUNTA function calculates how many of the values are non-blank. Any numeric or textual value will add to the count total. COUNTA is the Excel function equivalent to Lotus 1-2-3's PURECOUNT.

The COUNTIF function looks at a list of values, and calculates how many of them satisfy specified criteria.

An Excel database is a table or list of related data in an Excel spreadsheet that can be treated as a database of records.

The database function DSUM looks at a list or table of values, finds the rows that satisfy specified criteria, and adds up the values in a specified column of those rows.

DMIN finds the rows that satisfy specified criteria, and determines the minimum value in a specified column of those rows. Similarly, DMAX determines the maximum value in a specified column.

The DCOUNT function looks at a list or table of values, finds the rows that satisfy specified criteria, and counts them.

Quick Quiz

Circle the answer to each of the following multiple-choice questions about Excel's statistical and database functions.

Q1	The COUNT function counts...
A.	All cells in a range.
B.	All cells in a range containing numeric data.
C.	All cells in a range containing non-numeric data.
D.	All non-blank cells in a range.

Q2	The COUNTA function counts...
A.	All cells in a range containing text/alphabetic values.
B.	All non-blank cells in a range.
C.	All cells in a range.
D.	All cells in a range containing formula instead of absolute values.

Q3	An Excel database is...
A.	A cell range containing values imported from an external database.
B.	A type of Excel template.
C.	A table or list of related data in Excel.
D.	A dedicated worksheets in Excel that contains database information only.

Q4	In the DSUM function, you specify which column of data to sum by giving...
A.	The letter of the column on the worksheet.
B.	The number of the column on the worksheet (A=1, B=2, etc.).
C.	The number of the column in the Excel database cell range.
D.	The position of the column relative to the cell the formula is entered in (e.g. –2, +5, etc.).

Q5	The DCOUNT function counts cells containing...
A.	Numeric values.
B.	Non-numeric values.
C.	Non-blank values.
D.	Values satisfying specified criteria.

Answers   **1:** B; **2:** B; **3:** C; **4:** C; **5:** D.

Chapter 14: Using financial functions

In this chapter

So far in this book, you have learned about reference, mathematical, statistical and database functions in Excel.

Most of the time, Excel is used to keep track of financial information. Because of this, Excel also includes an extensive set of functions specifically designed to manipulate financial data. These functions calculate typical accounting figures, such as the future value of a series of investments at a fixed interest rate or the minimum interest rate required on an investment to achieve a target value in a specified time period.

In this chapter, you will learn how to use some of Excel's financial functions.

New skills

At the end of this chapter you should be able to:

- Use the NPV (Net Present Value) function
- Use the PV (Present Value) function
- Use the FV (Future Value) function
- Use the PMT (Payment) function
- Use the RATE function

New words

There are no new words in this chapter.

Syllabus reference

The following syllabus items are covered in this chapter:
- AM 4.3.1.5 – Use financial functions: FV; NPV; PMT; PV; RATE.

NPV

NPV is an Excel function that calculates the *Net Present Value* of an investment or debt. This gives the comparative value in today's terms of your investment or debt at the end of a period. For example, if inflation runs at 2.5%, then £1000 you own now will be worth comparatively less in 2 years time: the cost of the things you could buy with the £1000 goes up 2.5% each year, but unless it's invested wisely, your £1000 doesn't, so you can buy less with it at the end of the 2 years.

The NPV calculation allows you to determine the effect of influences such as inflation and depreciation on your assets or debts.

The financial function NPV has the following format:

=NPV(Rate, Value1, Value2, ...)	
Rate	The *discount* rate per period – that is, the rate at which your asset/liability devalues. This could be, for example, the inflation rate per period.
Value1, Value2, ...	A list of the payments made (negative numbers), and/or income earned (positive numbers) over the total investment period. The values can be of variable size, but must occur at regular intervals – if a payment is made *and* an income is earned at the end of each period, you should subtract the payment from the interest to calculate the value to use in this formula. The interval at which payments/income occur should be the same as the period of the discount rate, and payments/income are considered to apply from the *start* of each period.

MFPF put 10% of profits each month for the past year in a bank account with a negligible interest rate in order to save for improving their business facilities. Inflation for the year was 5.5%. Dividing this by 12, for simplicity, we get approximately 0.46% per month.

The total amount of money saved over the year was £2089.65. Taking inflation into account, if the Murphys could have predicted the NPV of their investment at the start of the 12-month period, what relative value could they have expected their £2089.65 to have?

In the next exercise you will calculate the NPV of MFPF's savings, relative to the start of the investment period.

Exercise 14.1: Using NPV

1. Open MFPF_FINANCE.XLS (or Ex12.10-OTYM1-MFPF_FINANCE.xls) and go to the *PROFIT* worksheet.
2. In cell *H1*, enter the label *Savings*.
3. In cell *H2*, enter the formula = *–D2*0.1*, to calculate 10% of the profit value in column D.
   The '–' is because the amounts are then paid into a savings account.
   Copy the formula to the other cells in the range *H2:H13*.
4. In cell *A18*, enter the label *Discount Rate*.
5. In cell *B18*, enter the formula *=0.055/12* to calculate the monthly rate of inflation.
6. In cell *A19*, enter the label *NPV*.
7. In cell *B19*, enter the formula *=NPV(B18,H2:H13)*.
   The result tells you that the NPV of the investment at the start of the year was £2034.93.

MFPF can buy £2089.65 worth of goods at the end of the year, using the money saved, but twelve months earlier, the same goods would have cost £2034.93. Prices have increased due to the 5.5% annual inflation rate.

A calculation like this might help the Murphys to decide whether they are better off taking out a loan at a particular interest rate to make a purchase immediately, or saving the full amount before making the purchase, although the comparative price of the purchase may be greater by the time they've finished saving.

PV

PV is an Excel function, similar to NPV, that calculates the *Present Value* of an investment where all the payments made are the same size and made at regular intervals. Unlike NPV where payments occurred at the start of each period, PV allows you to specify that they occur at the start *or* end of each period, but the timing must be the same for all payments over the total duration.

The financial function PV has the following format:

=PV(Rate, Nper, Pmt, Fv, Type)	
Rate	The discount rate per period.
Nper	The number of payment periods in the investment.
Pmt	The value of the payment made each period. This value cannot change over the lifetime of the investment. **Note:** You must either supply a value for *pmt* or for *fv*, but not both.
Fv	The future value the investment or debt should reach at maturity. If you are paying back a loan, the value of *fv* is 0. If you do not fill in a value, 0 is assumed. **Note:** You must either supply a value for *pmt* or for *fv*, but not both.
Type	1 or 0. 1 indicates that payment is made at the start of each period, and 0 that it is made at the end of the period. If you do not specify a value, 0 is assumed.

If MFPF had invested a consistent £150 each month instead of 10% of the month's profits, they would have saved £1800 over the year. Again, had they been able to predict at the start of the year what their investment would have been worth in relative terms at the end of the year, what would the PV of the £1800 have been?

In the next exercise you will calculate the PV at the start of the investment period of £150 savings per month over the 12-month period.

Exercise 14.2: Using PV

1. Open MFPF_FINANCE.XLS (or Ex14.1-MFPF_FINANCE.xls) and go to the *PROFIT* worksheet.
2. In cell *A20*, enter the label *Fixed sum*.
3. In cell *B20*, enter the value *–150*.
4. In cell *A21*, enter the label *PV*.
5. In cell *B21*, enter the formula *=PV(B18,12,B20)*.
   Cell *B18* contains the *rate* value, 12 is the number of payment periods, and cell *B20* contains the value for *pmt*. No values are specified for the *fv* or *type* parameters.
   The result tells you that the PV of the investment at the start of the year was £1747.50.

FV

FV is an Excel function used to calculate the future value of an investment or debt, where fixed payments are made at regular intervals. FV considers the interest rate being applied to the investment or debt and gives you an absolute value for the final worth of the investment, ignoring inflation and devaluation.

The financial function FV has the following format:

=FV(Rate, Nper, Pmt, Pv, Type)	
Rate	The interest rate per period.
Nper	The number of payment periods in the investment.
Pmt	The value of the payment made each period. This value cannot change over the lifetime of the investment. **Note:** You must either supply a value for *pmt* or for *pv*, but not both.

=FV(Rate, Nper, Pmt, Pv, Type)	
Pv	The present value of all of the future payments. If you do not fill in a value, *0* is assumed. **Note:** You must either supply a value for *pmt* or for *pv*, but not both.
Type	*1* or *0*. *1* indicates that payment is made at the start of each period, and *0* that it is made at the end of the period. If you do not specify a value, *0* is assumed.

The Murphys are considering opening a savings account that will pay 7.5% interest per annum provided at least £200 is deposited each month. If MFPF invests the minimum payment of £200 each month for 12 months, how much money will there be in the account, including interest?

In the next exercise, you will calculate how much money will be in the savings account at the end of a year if £200 is invested monthly.

Exercise 14.3: Using FV

1. Open MFPF_FINANCE.XLS (or Ex14.2-MFPF_FINANCE.xls) and go to the *PROFIT* worksheet.
2. In cell *A23*, enter the label *Fixed sum*.
3. In cell *B23*, enter the value *–200*.
4. In cell *A24*, enter the label *Interest rate*.
5. In cell *B24*, enter the formula *=0.075/12*.
6. In cell *A25*, enter the label *FV*.
7. In cell *B25*, enter the formula *=FV(B24, 12, B23)*.
Cell *B24* contains the *rate* value, 12 is the number of payment periods, and cell *B23* contains the value for *pmt*.
The result tells you that the future value of an account where £200 is invested each month for 12 months at an annual interest rate of 7.5%, is £2484.24.

PMT

You can use Excel's PMT function to calculate the size of fixed payments needed on an investment or debt, in order to reach a target value in a certain number of payments, where you already know the interest rate per period.

The financial function PMT has the following format:

=PMT(Rate, Nper, Pv, Fv, Type)	
Rate	The interest rate per period.
Nper	The number of payment periods in the investment.
Pv	The present value of all of the future payments combined. If you are calculating the size of payments to pay back a loan, this is the value of the loan. If you do not fill in a value, *0* is assumed.
Fv	The future value the investment or debt should reach at maturity. If you are paying back a loan, the value of *fv* is *0*. If you do not fill in a value, *0* is assumed.
Type	*1* or *0*. *1* indicates that payment is made at the start of each period, and *0* that it is made at the end of the period. If you do not specify a value, *0* is assumed.

Mr Murphy would like to buy a new delivery van. A local showroom has promised to sell him one used for display and test drives for the fixed price of £5500 at the end of next year. MFPF already has £2089.65 in savings from last year, so needs to save a further £3410.35 in the next 12 months to be able to buy the van.

Mr Murphy asks you to work out how much he would need to save each month in the account offering 7.5% interest per annum if he wanted to save *exactly* his shortfall of £3410.35 in 12 months, including interest.

In the next exercise, you will calculate the payment Mr Murphy must make into the savings account to achieve his target in 12 months.

Exercise 14.4: Using PMT

1. Open MFPF_FINANCE.XLS (or Ex14.3-MFPF_FINANCE.xls) and go to the *PROFIT* worksheet.
2. In cell *A26*, enter the label *PMT*.
3. In cell *B26*, enter the formula *=PMT(B24, 12, 0, 3410.35)*. Cell *B24* contains the interest rate value, 12 is the number of payment periods, 0 is the present value of the account, and £3410.35 is the target final value.
   The result tells you that MFPF needs to put £274.56 in the savings account each month to save £3410.35, including interest, by the end of the 12-month period.

RATE

RATE is an Excel financial function used to determine the interest rate on an investment where the number of payments and constant payment size are known, as well as either the PV or FV of the investment.

The financial function RATE has the following format:

=RATE(Nper, Pmt, Pv, Fv, Type, Guess)	
Nper	The number of payment periods in the investment.
Pmt	The value of the payment made each period. This value cannot change over the lifetime of the investment. **Note:** If you do not supply a value for *pmt*, you must supply one for *fv*.
Pv	The present value of all of the future payments combined. If you are calculating the size of payments to pay back a loan, this is the value of the loan. If you do not fill in a value, *0* is assumed.

=RATE(Nper, Pmt, Pv, Fv, Type, Guess)	
Fv	The future value the investment or debt should reach at maturity. If you are paying back a loan, the value of *fv* is *0*. If you do not fill in a value, *0* is assumed. **Note:** If you do not supply a value for *fv*, you must supply one for *pmt*.
Type	*1* or *0*. *1* indicates that payment is made at the start of each period, and *0* that it is made at the end of the period. If you do not specify a value, *0* is assumed.
Guess	Your guess for what you think the rate will be. This field can be left blank. If you do not supply a guess, 10% is assumed.

Mr Murphy has asked you to find out what interest rate an account should have for him to be able to save enough to pay for the new van by only investing £265 per month.

In the next exercise, you will work out the optimum interest rate for a savings account, so that the final amount in the account after 12 months will be £3410.35, including interest, when £265 is invested each month.

Exercise 14.5: Using RATE

1. Open MFPF_FINANCE.XLS (or Ex14.4-MFPF_FINANCE.xls) and go to the *PROFIT* worksheet.
2. In cell *A28*, enter the label *Rate*.
3. In cell *B28*, enter the formula =*RATE(12, –265, 0, 3410.35)*.
   The result tells you that Mr Murphy will need to find a savings account offering 1.26% interest per month (equivalent to 15.15% per annum), to achieve his target in 12 months.
   (You may need to apply cell formatting to see this result to two decimal places.)

Chapter summary

Excel's NPV function calculates the net present value of an investment or debt, where payments are at regular intervals, but of variable size. PV is similar to NPV, but calculates the present value of an investment where all the payments made are the same size and made at regular intervals.

FV calculates the future value of an investment or debt, where fixed payments are made at regular intervals.

PMT calculates the size of fixed payments needed on an investment or debt, in order to reach a target value in a certain number of payments, where you already know the interest rate per period.

RATE determines the interest rate on an investment where the number of payments and constant payment size are known, as well as either the PV or FV of the investment.

Quick Quiz

Circle the answer to each of the following multiple-choice questions about Excel's financial functions.

Q1	NPV stands for...
A.	New Payment Value.
B.	Net Payment Value.
C.	Net Present Value.
D.	Net Present Volume.

Q2	NPV and PV give the comparative value of an investment in current terms depending on factors such as... (Circle all that apply.)
A.	Inflation.
B.	Expansion.
C.	Depreciation.
D.	Coagulation.

Q3	In PMT(Rate, Nper, Pmt, Pv, Type) you *must* specify a value for Nper.
A.	True.
B.	False.

Q4	To calculate how much you should save regularly over a fixed period in order to achieve a target value at the end of the term, which financial function should you use?
A.	NPV.
B.	FV.
C.	PMT.
D.	RATE.

Q5	Investment amounts specified in the PV function must be made at the start of each period.
A.	True.
B.	False.

Answers   **1:** C; **2:** A, C; **3:** A; **4:** C; **5:** B.

Chapter 15: Using text and date functions

In this chapter

In general, you will use Excel spreadsheets to keep track of numeric information and to perform numeric calculations. But there are other types of data you can include in your spreadsheets – for example, text and dates.

Excel includes a number of functions that you can use to manipulate text and date information in your spreadsheets.

In this chapter you will learn how to manipulate text data, changing case, and creating concatenated strings.

You will also learn about the date functions in Excel, which allow you to generate and manipulate date information.

New skills

At the end of this chapter you should be able to:

- Use the PROPER, UPPER and LOWER text functions
- Use the CONCATENATE text function
- Use the TODAY date function
- Use the DAY, MONTH and YEAR date functions

New words

At the end of this chapter you should be able to explain the following terms:

- String

Syllabus reference

The following syllabus items are covered in this chapter:
- AM 4.3.1.1 – Use date and time functions: TODAY; DAY; MONTH; YEAR.
- AM 4.3.1.4 – Use text functions: PROPER; UPPER; LOWER; CONCATENATE.

Text functions

Earlier, you looked at functions, such as ROUND, that took numeric values as arguments, performed an operation on the value and displayed the result. There are also Excel functions which take text values as arguments, manipulate the text, and display the result.

In this chapter you will learn about text functions that allow you to change the case (upper or lower), and that allow you to combine text values into longer strings, and to combine text and numeric values into a single value.

> **String**
>
> *A string is a value that contains text, or text and numbers.*

Note: When using a string as an argument to a function in Excel, you must enclose it in double quotation marks ("....").

PROPER

PROPER is an Excel function which takes a string as an argument and capitalizes the first letter of each word.

In the next exercise, you will add a formula to a cell in PASTE_SPECIAL.XLS that retrieves the string in another cell, reformats it with the first letter of each word capitalized, and displays the result.

Exercise 15.1: Using PROPER

1. Open PASTE_SPECIAL.XLS (or Ex6.11-paste_special.xls).
2. In cell *A28*, enter the formula *=PROPER(A12)*.
   The text from cell *A12* is now shown in cell *A28*, reformatted so that the first letter of each word is capitalized.

UPPER

UPPER is an Excel function which takes a string as an argument and capitalizes every letter.

In the next exercise, you will add a formula to another cell in PASTE_SPECIAL.XLS (or Ex15.1-paste_special.xls) that will retrieve the PROPER case string you generated in *Exercise 15.1*, and reformat it with every letter capitalized.

Exercise 15.2: Using UPPER

1. Open PASTE_SPECIAL.XLS (or Ex15.1-paste_special.xls).
2. In cell *A29*, enter the formula =*UPPER(A28)*.
   The text from cell *A28* is shown in cell *A29*, reformatted so that every letter is capitalized.

LOWER

LOWER is an Excel function which takes a string as an argument and changes every letter to lower case.

In the next exercise, you will add a formula to another cell in PASTE_SPECIAL.XLS, retrieve the UPPER case string you generated in *Exercise 15.2*, and reformat it with every letter in lower case.

Exercise 15.3: Using LOWER

1. Open PASTE_SPECIAL.XLS (or Ex15.2-paste_special.xls).
2. In cell *A30*, enter the formula =*LOWER(A29)*.
   The text from cell *A29* is shown in cell *A30*, reformatted so that every letter is in lower case.

Reusing text values in longer strings

Sometimes, you may want to join values together in a spreadsheet to create new strings. For example, say a spreadsheet listing staff members has first names in column *A*, and surnames in column *B*. You could join the values from the cells in columns *A* and *B* in each row together to generate full names.

Joining a series of text strings together is known as concatenation, and Excel has a text function, CONCATENATE, which can do just that.

CONCATENATE

CONCATENATE is an Excel function which takes a series of arguments separated by commas and joins them together to create a single string. Arguments can be cell references, numbers or text.

Note: When using CONCATENATE, you must include any spaces you want to appear between concatenated terms. The spaces should appear inside quotation marks, or they will be ignored. Space is not added automatically between arguments.

In the next exercise, you will use the CONCATENATE function to join two strings and the value from a cell together to create a new string.

Exercise 15.4: Using CONCATENATE

1. Open PASTE_SPECIAL.XLS (or Ex15.3-paste_special.xls).
2. In cell *A32*, enter the formula =*CONCATENATE("The text in cell A12 says: ",A12,"!!")* and press **ENTER**.
   The value in cell A32 is now: *The text in cell A12 says: yOuR vAlUe HeRe:!!*
3. Save and close your workbook when you are done.

Date

Excel's date functions allow you to generate and manipulate date information. In this chapter you will look at formulae which allow you to automatically retrieve the current day's date, and to select individual elements of a date to show, such as the month.

TODAY

TODAY is an Excel date function that returns the current date. This function can be a useful timesaver, as you neither have to find the current date nor type it in.

In the next exercise you will edit the invoice template, INVOICE_MFPF.XLT (or Ex2.2-INVOICE_MFPF.xlt), and add the TODAY function to automatically fill in the date an invoice is edited.

Note: When you have finished writing an invoice, you should use **Copy** and **Paste Special** to replace the date formula with the value it generates. Otherwise, the next time you open the document to read or edit, the date will be updated again.

Exercise 15.5: Using TODAY

1. Create a new spreadsheet based on the INVOICE_MFPF.XLT (or Ex2.2-INVOICE_MFPF.xlt) template.
2. In cell *F5*, enter the formula =*TODAY()*.
3. Save the spreadsheet as a template, replacing the original INVOICE_MFPF.XLT.

DAY, MONTH and YEAR

DAY, MONTH, and YEAR are Excel functions that take a date as an argument, and return the number value of the day, month and year portions of that date respectively.

In the next exercise, you will use CONCATENATE in conjunction with DAY, MONTH and YEAR to create a sentence which lists the number values for the day, month and year of the date generated by TODAY.

Exercise 15.6: Using DAY, MONTH and YEAR

1. Open a new blank spreadsheet.
2. In cell *A1*, enter the label *Today's date*.
3. In cell *A2*, enter the formula =*TODAY()*.
   In cell *C1*, enter the formula =*CONCATENATE("Today is day ",DAY(A2)," of month ",MONTH(A2),", ",YEAR(A2),".")*.
4. Close the workbook *without saving* when finished.

Chapter summary

A string is a value that contains text, or text and numbers.

The PROPER text function takes a string as an argument and capitalizes the first letter of each word. UPPER capitalizes every letter, and LOWER reformats the text so that every letter is in lower case.

CONCATENATE takes a series of strings and joins them all together to create a single string. Strings can be cell references, numbers or text.

The TODAY date function returns the current date. The DAY, MONTH and YEAR functions take a date as an argument, and return the number value of the day, month and year portions of that date respectively.

Quick Quiz

Circle the answer to each of the following multiple-choice questions about Excel's text and date functions.

Q1	The PROPER function takes a text argument and...
A.	Checks it for proper spelling.
B.	Capitalizes the first letter of the first word in the string and changes all other letters in the string to lower case.
C.	Capitalizes the first letter of every word in the string.
D.	Capitalizes the first letter of proper nouns in the string only.

Q2	String arguments for text functions must be enclosed by...
A.	Quotation marks – " ".
B.	Brackets – ( ).
C.	Dollar signs – $ $.
D.	Hash signs – # #.

Q3	The UPPER function changes which parts of a string to upper case:
A.	All letters.
B.	First letter in each sentence.
C.	First letter in each word.
D.	Only letters that start off as lower case.

Q4	Strings passed as arguments to text functions cannot contain numeric values.
A.	True.
B.	False.

Q5	The CONCATENATE function automatically adds a blank space between each argument when it sticks them together.
A.	True.
B.	False.

Answers **1:** C; **2:** A; **3:** A; **4:** B; **5:** B.

Chapter 16: Using logical functions

In this chapter

Earlier, you learned how to apply formatting to a cell if the value it contained satisfied certain criteria (conditional formatting). Sometimes, you may want to check whether a value satisfies certain criteria and do something else if it does, but not do anything to the actual data.

For example, you might want to check if your profits for any month are below a certain value for your own information, but not apply any distinctive formatting to the value. Otherwise it will be the first thing a bank manager or prospective investor notices when looking at your accounts!

Excel's logical functions allow you to check the values of data against certain criteria. The functions return a value of TRUE if the criteria are satisfied, and FALSE if they are not.

New skills

At the end of this chapter you should be able to:

- Use the IF function
- Use the AND and OR functions
- Use the ISERROR function

New words

There are no new words in this chapter.

Syllabus reference

The following syllabus items are covered in this chapter:
- AM 4.3.1.7 – Use logical functions: IF; AND; OR; ISERROR.

ECDL Advanced Spreadsheets for Microsoft® Office XP and 2003

IF

Excel's logical functions are used to check if the value in a cell satisfies certain criteria. They return a value of *TRUE* if it does, and *FALSE* if it does not.

You can use Excel's IF function to perform a logical test and return custom messages for *TRUE* and *FALSE* results. The logical test can be any comparison using the expressions <, >, =, <= (which means less than or equal to) or >= (which means greater than or equal to), and can include cell references as well as numeric and text values. The logical test can even be another logical function, for example an AND comparison.

The logical function IF has the following format:

IF(Logical_test, Value_if_true, Value_if_false)	
Logical_test	The logical test or comparison to perform, for example, *A1>B1*.
Value_if_true	The value to return if the result of the logical test is *TRUE*. If the value is a string, it should be enclosed in quotation marks, for example, *"Passed Test"*. The default value, used if you don't specify an alternative, is *TRUE*.
Value_if_false	The value to return if the result of the logical test is *FALSE*. If the value is a string, it should be enclosed in quotation marks, for example, *"Failed Test"*. The default value, used if you don't specify an alternative, is *FALSE*.

Mrs Murphy has asked you to indicate, beside the profit figure for each month, whether the profits have gone up or down from the previous month.

In the next exercise you will use the IF function to compare the profit figure for each month with the one for the previous month. You will return a message of *UP* if a month's profit is greater than the profit for the previous month, and *DOWN* if it is less than the profit for the previous month.

Exercise 16.1: Using IF

1. Open MFPF_FINANCE.XLS (or Ex14.4-MFPF_FINANCE.xls) and go to the *PROFIT* worksheet.
2. Select column F, where you calculated rounded profit using a single formula, and delete its contents.
3. In cell *F1*, enter the label *TREND*.
4. In cell *F3*, enter the formula *=IF(D3>D2,"UP","DOWN")*.
5. Copy the formula to the other cells in the range *F3:F13*.
   As you do not have a profit value for the previous December to compare with the January value, you should not enter a formula in cell *F2*.
6. Save your workbook when you are done.

Over to you: mandatory

In the invoice template, INVOICE_MFPF.XLT (or Ex15.5-INVOICE_MFPF.xlt), the white text *Late* in cell *D9* on the *PERSONAL NOTES* worksheet is conditionally formatted in red if the customer pays more than 28 days after the invoice was issued. If you changed the fill colour of cell *D9* to any other colour, the white text would be visible. Use the IF function to generate the *Late* text instead.

- Create a new spreadsheet based on the template INVOICE_MFPF.XLT you edited earlier (or Ex15.5-INVOICE_MFPF.xlt).
- Delete the text in cell *D9* on the *Personal Notes* worksheet, and change the text colour for the cell back to black.
- Add an IF function to the cell which checks if the difference between *Date Paid* and *Date Invoiced* is greater than 28, returns the text *Late* if it is, and no message otherwise.
- Save the spreadsheet as a template, replacing the original INVOICE_MFPF.XLT.

AND

AND is an Excel function that examines a list of logical tests or comparisons, and returns a value of *TRUE* if *all* of the logical tests are true. Otherwise, the function returns a value of *FALSE*.

The logical function AND has the following format:

AND(Logical1, Logical2, ...)	
Logical1, Logical2, ...	The list of logical tests or comparisons to perform.

To return a custom message instead of TRUE or FALSE, you could nest this function in an IF function, as the *Logical_test* argument.

For example, the formula
=*IF(AND(B1<2,B2<2),"Both < 2","Not both < 2")*
returns the string *Both < 2* if the values in both cells *B1* and *B2* are less than 2, making the AND function return *TRUE*, and returns the string *Not both < 2* if the AND function returns *FALSE*.

Mr Murphy is wondering if he should sell garden tables and garden chairs packaged together as sets. He asks you to look at the orders for the last year to see if customers usually buy both garden chairs and garden tables at the same time.

In the next exercise, you will use the logical AND function to find the orders where both garden chairs and garden tables were ordered at the same time.

Exercise 16.2: Using AND

1. Open MFPF_ORD.XLS (or Ex13.7-MFPF_ORD.xls) and go to the *COMPLETE* worksheet.
2. In cell *K1*, enter the label *Chairs and Tables*.
3. In cell *K2*, enter the formula =*AND(I2>0,J2>0)*.
4. Copy the formula to the other cells in column K.
   The message *TRUE* appears in the rows where both garden chairs and garden tables were ordered.
   The message *FALSE* appears where either no garden chairs or garden tables were ordered, or where only one or the other were ordered.

OR

OR is an Excel function that examines a list of logical tests or comparisons, and returns a value of *TRUE* if one or more of the logical tests are true. Otherwise, the function returns a value of *FALSE*.

The logical function OR has the following format:

OR(Logical1, Logical2, ...)	
Logical1, Logical2, ...	The list of logical tests or comparisons to perform.

The results in column *K* show which customer bought both garden tables and garden chairs. Next, you will see who bought garden tables or garden chairs or both, using the OR function. By comparing the values, you will be able to see who bought one but not the other.

In the next exercise, you will use the OR function to check which customers ordered either garden chairs or garden tables or both.

Exercise 16.3: Using OR

1. Open MFPF_ORD.XLS (or Ex16.2-MFPF_ORD.xls) and go to the *COMPLETE* worksheet.
2. In cell *L1*, enter the label *Chair and/or Tables*.
3. In cell *L2*, enter the formula *=OR(I2>0,J2>0)*.
4. Copy the formula to the other cells in column *L*.
   Orders where either garden chairs or garden tables were ordered, as well as orders where both garden chairs and garden tables were ordered, are now flagged as *TRUE* in column *L*.

Over to you: mandatory

On the *COMPLETE* worksheet of MFPF_ORD.XLS (or Ex16.3-MFPF_ORD.xls), by looking at columns *K* and *L* together, you can see which customers bought either garden chairs or garden tables but not both of them. You could see this information more clearly if you used another logical function to compare the results of both tests.

- In column *M*, use an AND function to flag the orders with a *FALSE* value in column *K*, and a *TRUE* value in column *L*. A *TRUE* result in column *M* indicates an order where either chairs or tables but not both were bought.

Over to you: optional

You could also construct a nested function to perform this check in a single step.

- Create an AND function that uses an AND and an OR function as arguments to determine which customers bought either garden chairs or garden tables, but not both.

ISERROR

ISERROR is an Excel function that examines the value in a cell, and returns a value of *TRUE* if the value is an Excel error message. Otherwise, the function returns a value of *FALSE*.

The information function ISERROR has the following format:

ISERROR(Value)	
Value	The cell to check for an error message.

You have decided to add a worksheet to MFPF_FINANCE.XLS which will contain ISERROR checks for all of the formulae used in the workbook. This means that when you make changes to the data in your workbook, you can see quickly and easily if your changes contravene any of the formulae you use just by looking at this one sheet.

In the next exercise, you will add a new worksheet to MFPF_FINANCE.XLS (or Ex16.1-MFPF_FINANCE.xls) and start adding ISERROR checks for cells containing formulae.

Exercise 16.4: Using ISERROR

1. Open MFPF_FINANCE.XLS (or Ex16.1-MFPF_FINANCE.xls) and add a new worksheet.

Name the new worksheet *Errors*.

2. In cell *A1*, enter the label *NPV*.
3. In cell *B1*, enter the formula *=ISERROR(PROFIT!B19)*.
   The value is *FALSE* because there is no error in cell *B19* on the *PROFIT* worksheet.

Over to you: optional

If you would like to reassure yourself that the ISERROR function really works, go to the *PROFIT* worksheet and edit the NPV formula to say *=NPV(I2,E2:E13)/0*. This generates a *#DIV/0!* error, and changes the value in cell B1 on the *Errors* worksheet to *TRUE*.

Chapter summary

Excel's logical functions are used to check if the value in a cell satisfies certain criteria. They return a value of *TRUE* if it does, and *FALSE* if it does not.

IF performs a logical test and can return custom messages for *TRUE* and *FALSE* results.

AND examines a list of logical tests or comparisons, and returns a value of *TRUE* if *all* of the logical tests are true. OR returns a value of *TRUE* if one or more of the logical tests are true.

ISERROR examines the value in a cell, and returns a value of *TRUE* if the value is an Excel error message.

Quick Quiz

Circle the answer to each of the following multiple-choice questions about Excel's logical functions.

Q1	If you don't specify a Value_if_false argument for the IF(Logical_test, Value_if_true, Value_if_false) function, then if the result of the test is false...
A.	The function won't display any result.
B.	The function will generate an error.
C.	The function will return *FALSE*.
D.	The function will use the *Value_if_true* argument instead.

Q2	All logical functions allow you to specify a custom message instead of TRUE or FALSE.
A.	True.
B.	False.

Q3	The AND function takes exactly two logical tests as arguments.
A.	True.
B.	False.

Q4	Logical functions can be nested in other functions.
A.	True.
B.	False.

Q5	The ISERROR function is used to highlight cells containing errors by formatting them in a particular way.
A.	True.
B.	False.

Answers **1:** C; **2:** B; **3:** B; **4:** A; **5:** B.

Chapter 17: Using data tables and scenarios

In this chapter

What if you invested in a savings account with a 4% interest rate instead of one with a 3% interest rate? You'd earn more money – but how much more exactly? What if you invested £170 per month instead of £150? Would the extra interest make up for having £20 less to spend each month? What effect would one or more of these changes have on the value of your savings in 6 months or a year's time?

To answer questions like these, where you have several alternative options – in this case different lodgement amounts or investment periods – you could use for arguments in a calculation and want to know what the result of the calculation would be if you used each of them, you could create a formula for each possibility and enter it in your spreadsheet.

Aside from this method, Excel offers you two quick and handy ways to deal with such 'What-if?' calculations: data tables and scenarios.

In this chapter you will learn how to use each of these tools.

New skills

At the end of this chapter you should be able to:

- Use a 1-input data table
- Use a 2-input data table
- Create a named scenario
- View a named scenario
- Generate a scenario summary report

New words

At the end of this chapter you should be able to explain the following terms:

- Data table
- Scenario

Syllabus reference

The following syllabus items are covered in this chapter:

- AM 4.1.2.5 – Use one-input or two-input Data tables / What-if tables.
- AM 4.4.2.1 – Create named Scenarios / Versions from defined cell ranges.
- AM 4.4.2.2 – Create a Scenario summary / Version report.

Data tables

In *Chapter 14: Using financial functions*, you calculated how much money Mr Murphy needed to save each month in an account with a particular interest rate to have saved a target amount at the end of 12 months. Then you calculated what interest rate an account would need to attract for him to be able to save a smaller amount each month and reach the same goal.

You could have created a data table to find the ideal combination of RATE and PMT values to achieve a target FV result.

> **Data table**
>
> *A data table is a range of cells that shows the results of substituting different values in one or more formulae.*

There are two types of data table:

- 1-input data table: In a 1-input data table, you can substitute different values for *one* variable, and see the effect each value has on the results of *one or more* formulae.
- 2-input data table: In a 2-input data table, you can substitute different values for *two* variables, and see the effect each variable value combination has on *a single* formula.

1-input data tables

With a 1-input data table, you can see the effect that changing a single variable value has on the results of any number of formulae that use that value. You could use a 1-input data table to work out the future value a fixed savings investment would have for a range of different interest rates, for example.

A 1-input data table lists the possible values for the changing variable on one axis, and a series of formulae that use that value on the other axis. Excel completes the data table by filling in the results for each of the formulae using the different variable values.

In the following example, a 1-input data table has been set up with a list of possible interest rates in a column orientation, and an FV formula in a row orientation. Results have not yet been calculated.

The FV formula will be used to calculate the possible future values of an investment of a fixed sum of £200 over 12 payment periods. Initially, the FV formula takes the interest rate value from cell *B1*. To fill in the data table with the value of FV for each interest rate, you must tell Excel to replace the value in cell *B1* with the values in the column axis of the table.

	A	B	C	D
1	Interest rate per period	0.0025		
2				
3			=FV(B1,12,-200)	
4		0.0025		
5	Interest rates	0.005		
6		0.0075		
7		0.01		
8		0.0125		
9		0.015		
10				

The formulae refer to a specific cell on the worksheet, but the value in that cell is actually replaced by each variable value on the other axis of the table to calculate the final results.

Note: If you enter your variables in a *column* orientation, you should add your first formula in the cell one column to the right of, and one row above, the cell containing the first variable value. Any other formulae should be entered in the cells to the right of the first formula.
If you enter your variable in a *row* orientation, you should add your first formula in the cell one column to the left of, and one row below, the cell containing the first variable value. Any other formulae should be entered in the cells below the first formula.

In the next exercise, you will create the 1-input data table shown in the example, and fill in the final results.

Exercise 17.1: Using a 1-input data table

1. Create a new worksheet, based on the default template, and save it as INVEST.XLS.
2. In cell *A1* of the first worksheet, enter the label *Interest rate per period*.
3. In cell *B1*, enter the value *0.0025* - a quarter of one percent.
4. In cell *A4*, enter the label *Interest Rates*.
5. Change the formatting of cell *A4* so that the text in it is bold and rotated by 90 degrees, then merge and centre the cell range *A4:A9*.
6. In the cell range *B4:B9*, enter the variable values *0.0025*, *0.005*, *0.0075*, *0.01*, *0.0125* and *0.015*.
   These are the variable values you will substitute in place of the interest rate in cell *B1*.
7. In cell *C3*, enter the formula *=FV(B1,12,–200)*.
8. Select the range *B3:C9*, and select **Data | Table...**.
   The *Table* dialog box opens.

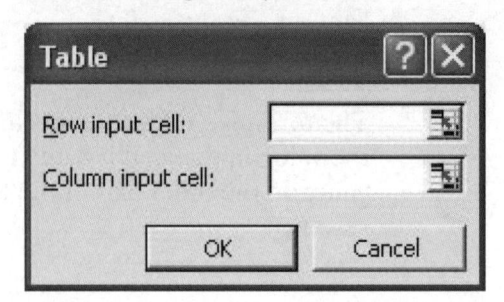

9. In this dialog box, you will tell Excel which cell referred to in your formulae should be replaced by the variable values in either the column or row orientation in your data table.
   Enter the cell *B1* in the *Column input cell* field.
   Click **OK**.
   The data table is filled in with the values calculated for FV with each possible interest rate.

	A	B	C	D
1	Interest rate per period	0.0025		
2				
3			2433.276553	
4		0.0025	2433.276553	
5	Interest rates	0.005	2467.112475	
6		0.0075	2501.517271	
7		0.01	2536.500603	
8		0.0125	2572.072284	
9		0.015	2608.242286	
10				

(You may need to apply additional cell formatting to see your results to the same number of decimal places shown in the illustration.)

10. Save your workbook when you are done.

2-input data tables

You can also create a 2-input data table to calculate the possible results of a *single* formula where the values of two of the inputs can change. For example, to calculate FV for a potential investment, if there are a variety of interest rates to choose from, and several possible values for the regular PMT amount you contribute to the investment, you could create a 2-input data table.

In this case, one set of variables is entered in the row orientation of the data table, and the other in the column orientation – because both axes of the table are used for variables, you can only specify *one* formula to use to complete the table.

The formula should be entered in the cell immediately above the first entry in the column of variable values, and the row of variable values should be entered in the cell range starting with the first cell to the right of the formula.

In the next exercise, you will create a 2-input data table which calculates the value of FV where both the interest rate per period and the payment amount are variables.

Exercise 17.2: Using a 2-input data table

1. In cell *C1* of the first worksheet in INVEST.xls (or Ex17.1-INVEST.xls), enter the label *Payment*.
2. In cell *D1*, enter the value *–150*.
3. In cell *A11*, enter the formula *=FV(B1,12,D1)*.
   Cell *B1* contains the value for *rate*, 12 is the number of payment periods, and cell *D1* contains the value for *pmt* (the payment amount).
4. In the cell range *A12:A17*, enter the variable values *0.0025, 0.005, 0.0075, 0.01, 0.0125* and *0.015*.
   These are the variable values you will substitute for the interest rate in cell *B1*.
5. In the cell range *B11:G11*, enter the variable values *–150, –160, –170, –180, –190* and *–200*.
   These are the variable values you will substitute for the payment amount in cell *D1*.
6. Select the cell range *A11:G17* and select **Data | Table...**.
   The *Table* dialog box opens.
7. In the *Column Input Cell* field, enter *B1*.
   In the *Row Input Cell* field, enter *D1*.
   Click **OK**.
   The data table is filled in with the values calculated for FV with each interest rate and payment amount combination.

	A	B	C	D	E	F	G	H
1	Interest rate per period	0.0025	payment	-150				
2								
3			€2,433.28					
4		0.0025	2433.276553					
5	interest rates	0.005	2467.112475					
6		0.0075	2501.517271					
7		0.01	2536.500603					
8		0.0125	2572.072284					
9		0.015	2608.242286					
10								
11	€1,824.96	-150	-160	-170	-180	-190	-200	
12	0.0025	1824.957	1946.621242	2068.285	2189.949	2311.613	2433.277	
13	0.005	1850.334	1973.68998	2097.046	2220.401	2343.757	2467.112	
14	0.0075	1876.138	2001.213817	2126.29	2251.366	2376.441	2501.517	
15	0.01	1902.375	2029.200482	2156.026	2282.851	2409.676	2536.501	
16	0.0125	1929.054	2057.657827	2186.261	2314.865	2443.469	2572.072	
17	0.015	1956.182	2086.593829	2217.006	2347.418	2477.83	2608.242	
18								

8. Save your workbook when you are done.

Named scenarios

What if you wanted to substitute different values for the third variable for the number of payment periods in the FV formula too? You cannot do this in a data table, but you can use Excel's **Scenarios** functionality to substitute values for any number of variables.

> **Scenario**
>
> *A scenario is a named set of values that can be substituted into a set of selected cells in a spreadsheet.*

When you create a scenario, you define a set of values that should be entered in particular cells on a worksheet, and assign a name to that scenario. You can select any one scenario to view at one time, and all the defined values in that scenario are substituted into your worksheet.

Creating a scenario

In the next exercise, you will create a scenario that specifies a particular combination of values for the number of payment periods in an investment, the payment amount per period, and the interest rate per period.

Exercise 17.3: Creating a named scenario

1. In cell *E1* of the first worksheet in INVEST.xls (or Ex17.2-INVEST.xls), enter the label *Payment Periods*.
2. In cell *F1*, enter the value *12*.
3. In cell *A2*, enter the label *FV*.
4. In cell *B2*, enter the formula *=FV(B1,F1,D1)*.
   Cell *B1* contains the value for *rate*, cell *F1* contains the value for *nper* (the number of payment periods), and cell *D1* contains the value for *pmt*.
5. Select **Tools | Scenarios...**.
   The *Scenario Manager* dialog box opens.
6. Click **Add...**.
   The *Add Scenario* dialog box opens.

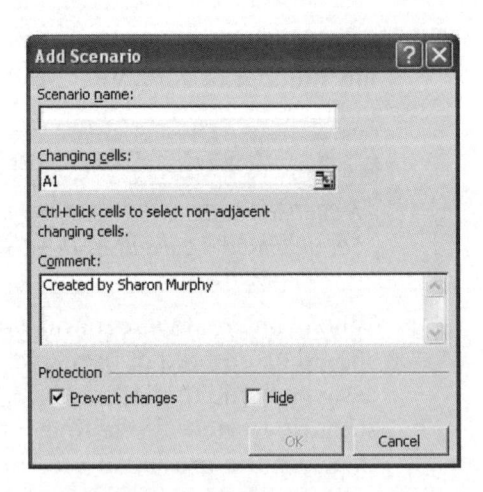

7. In the *Scenario name* field, enter *Savings1*.
   In the *Changing cells* field, enter *B1,D1,F1*.
   Click **OK**.
   The *Scenario Values* dialog box opens.

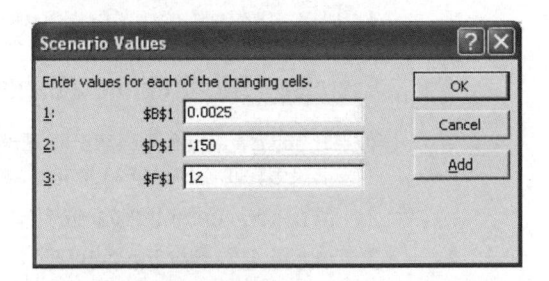

8. In the *Scenario Values* dialog box, the current values in the selected cells are shown.
   You can edit one or more of these values, and save all three in the current scenario by clicking **OK**.
   For now, you will save the default values in the *Savings1* scenario.

9. Click **OK**.

10. Click **Close** to close the *Scenario Manager* dialog box.

Over to you: mandatory

In INVEST.xls (or Ex17.3-INVEST.xls), continue to add scenarios using different combinations of values for interest rate per period in cell B1, number of periods in the investment in cell F1, and payment amount per period in cell D1. Add at least two more scenarios.

Viewing a scenario

When you have defined your scenarios, you can select any one of them to view. All of the scenario values you defined are filled in to the selected changing cells, and the results of any formulae that use these cells are updated.

Exercise 17.4: Viewing a scenario

1. Open INVEST.xls (or Ex17.3-OTYM1-INVEST.xls).
2. Select **Tools | Scenarios...**.
   The *Scenario Manager* dialog box opens.
3. In the *Scenarios* area, select one of the two additional scenarios you defined and click **Show**.
4. Click **Close** to close the *Scenario Manager* dialog box.
   The values for cells B1, D1 and F1 specified in the scenario are substituted into the worksheet and the result of the formula in cell B2 changes to reflect the new values in cells B1, D1 and F1.
5. Save your workbook when you are done.

Scenario summaries

Unlike data tables, which show all possible results at once, you can only see the data for one scenario at a time. This makes it difficult to compare the effect each set of values has just by looking at the results.

Excel allows you to create scenario summary reports which show the set of values defined in each scenario, and also the final numbers in selected results cells on the worksheet that rely on the variable values.

In the next exercise, you will create a summary report which shows the settings for, and results of, each scenario you have defined on the first worksheet of INVEST.XLS.

Exercise 17.5: Creating a scenario summary

1. Open INVEST.xls (or Ex17.4-INVEST.xls).
2. Select **Tools | Scenarios...**.
3. Click **Summary...**.
   The *Scenario Summary* dialog box opens.

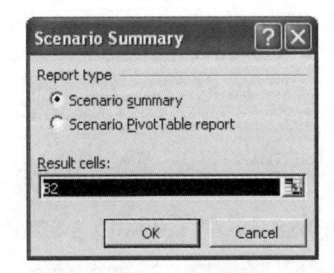

4. In the *Report type* area, select *Scenario summary*.
5. In the *Result cells* area, enter *$B$2*.
   This is the cell that contains the FV formula that uses the data from the changing cells.
6. Click **OK**.
7. A new worksheet is added to your workbook.
   The worksheet contains a summary report of the scenarios you defined. It shows the changing cells and their values for each scenario, as well as the results cells and their values.

Scenario Summary	Current Values:	Savings1	Savings2	Savings3
Changing Cells:				
$B$1	0.0025	0.0025	0.005	0.0025
$D$1	-150	-150	-150	-200
$F$1	12	12	18	12
Result Cells:				
$B$2	1824.957415	1824.957415	2817.868187	2433.276553

Notes: Current Values column represents values of changing cells at time Scenario Summary Report was created. Changing cells for each scenario are highlighted in gray.

8. Save and close your workbook when you are done.

Chapter summary

A data table is a range of cells that shows the results of substituting different values in one or more formulae.

There are two types of data table:

- 1-input data table: In a 1-input data table, you can substitute different values for one variable, and see the effect each value has on the results of one or more formulae.
- 2-input data table: In a 2-input data table, you can substitute different values for two variables, and see the

effect each variable value combination has on a single formula.

A scenario is a named set of values that can be substituted into a set of selected cells in a spreadsheet. You can only view one scenario at a time.

You can create scenario summary reports which show the set of values defined in each scenario, and also the final numbers in selected results cells on the worksheet that rely on the variable values.

Quick Quiz

Circle the answer to each of the following multiple-choice questions about data tables and scenarios in Excel.

Q1	A 2-input data table lets you substitute multiple values for two variables in a number of formulae.
A.	True.
B.	False.

Q2	It is not possible to substitute values for more than 2 variables in Excel calculations.
A.	True.
B.	False.

Q3	You can only view one scenario at a time.
A.	True.
B.	False.

Q4	A scenario summary shows...
A.	The values in the changing and result cells of the current scenario.
B.	The values in the changing and result cells of a selected subset of scenarios.
C.	The values in the changing and result cells of all scenarios.
D.	A list of names of all defined scenarios only.

Q5	When you select a scenario and click Show, Excel updates all result cells dependent on the scenario inputs.
A.	True.
B.	False.

Answers **1:** B; **2:** B; **3:** A; **4:** C; **5:** A.

Chapter 18: Auditing your spreadsheets

In this chapter

Congratulations! Your workbooks are now completed. You have entered or imported all of the required data, and you have made all of your calculations.

But now that you've added all that data, you're faced with the problem of figuring out which cells contain pure values, and which contain formulae? Also, which cells are used by which formulae? How can you tell what you can edit directly, and what you should leave alone in case you break something somewhere else in your spreadsheet?

In this chapter, you will learn how to audit your worksheets to locate the cells containing formulae, and to track which cells contain values used in formulae, and which cells contain the formulae that use them.

New skills

At the end of this chapter you should be able to:

- Locate and display formulae on a worksheet
- Trace precedent and dependent cells

New words

There are no new words in this chapter.

Syllabus reference

The following syllabus items are covered in this chapter:
- AM 4.4.3.1 – Trace precedent cells in a worksheet.
- AM 4.4.3.2 – Trace dependent cells in a worksheet.
- AM 4.4.3.3 – Display all formulas or view location of all formulas in a worksheet.

Formulae and locations

In *Exercise 16.4* on page 188, you started to add ISERROR functions to a worksheet which would check selected formulae in your workbook for errors. But, how can you tell which cells in your worksheets contain formulae, without checking each and every cell individually?

Excel allows you to identify the cells in a worksheet that contain formulae in two ways:

- Using the **Go To** command to select all the cells that contain formulae.
- Choosing to display the formulae in cells, instead of the values they generate.

Go To

In the next exercise, you will use Excel's **Go To** command to select all of the cells on the *PROFIT* worksheet of MFPF_FINANCE.XLS (or Ex16.4-MFPF_FINANCE.xls) that contain formulae.

Exercise 18.1: Highlighting cells that contain formulae

1. Open MFPF_FINANCE.XLS (or Ex16.4-MFPF_FINANCE.xls) and go to the *PROFIT* worksheet.
2. Make sure that only one cell on the worksheet is selected – if you select a cell range, the next step will apply to that cell range rather than to the complete worksheet.
3. Select **Edit | Go To...**.
   The *Go To* dialog box opens.
   This dialog box lists named cell ranges on the current worksheet.

4. Click **Special...**.
 The *Go To Special* dialog box opens.

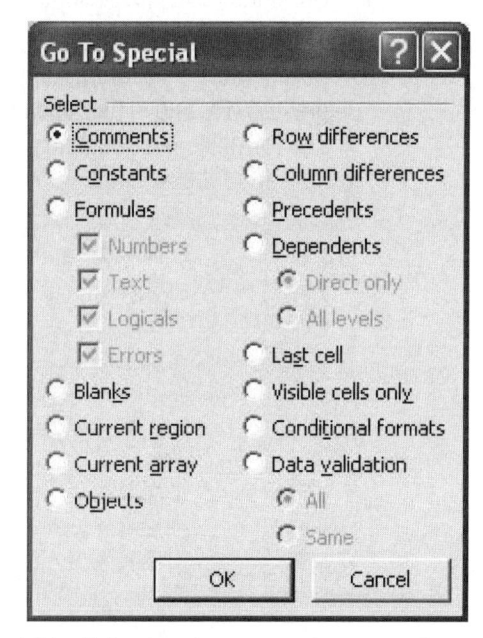

 This dialog box lets you select a particular cell property that the cells you want to select have.
 If you click **OK**, then any cell with the selected property is selected.
 If multiple cells have the property, they are all selected.

5. Select *Formulas*, and ensure that all of the different formula types are selected.

6. Click **OK**.
 All of the cells on the *PROFIT* worksheet that contain formulae are now selected.

You can select all cells containing formulae using **Go To**, but to see the actual formula in a given cell, you need to select that cell and read the formula from the formula bar. When you do this, you deselect all of the other cells again.

Displaying formulae

You can specify that you want to show all formulae in a worksheet instead of the values they generate.

In the next exercise, you will display all of the formulae in the *INCOMING* worksheet of MFPF_FINANCE.XLS (or Ex18.1-MFPF_FINANCE.xls).

Exercise 18.2: Showing formulae instead of values

1. Go to the *INCOMING* worksheet of MFPF_FINANCE.XLS (or Ex18.1-MFPF_FINANCE.xls).

2. Select **Tools | Formula Auditing | Formula Auditing Mode** or press **CTRL** and ` (the open single inverted comma key). The formulae used to calculate values on this sheet are shown instead of the values.

	A	B	C	D
1		Products	Delivery	
2	Jan	6720	25	
3	Feb	3175	20	
4	Mar	2590	30	
5	Apr	2355	20	
6	May	5900	40	
7	Jun	5335	50	
8	Jul	6780	55	
9	Aug	5955	40	
10	Sep	2330	35	
11	Oct	1905	20	
12	Nov	4190	30	
13	Dec	2630	20	
14				
15	Annual Total:		=SUM(Products)+SUM(Delivery)	
16				

You can toggle between formulae and values by pressing **CTRL** and ' repeatedly.

Tracing precedent cells

Without reading the list of arguments for a formula, how can you tell which cells it gets data from?

Excel's **Trace Precedents** command locates all of the cells referred to by the formula in a selected cell, and connects them to the cell containing the formula using arrows.

If any of the precedent cells are not on the same worksheet as the selected cell, a spreadsheet icon is shown at the other end of the precedent's arrow. You should examine the formula in the selected cell to determine what worksheet the precedent cells are on.

In the next exercise you will use the **Trace Precedents** command to indicate the cells which contain input data for the NPV formula on the *PROFIT* worksheet of MFPF_FINANCE.XLS (or Ex18.2-MFPF_FINANCE.xls).

Exercise 18.3: Tracing precedent cells

1. Open MFPF_FINANCE.XLS (or Ex18.2-MFPF_FINANCE.xls) and go to the *PROFIT* worksheet.
2. Select cell *B19*, which contains the NPV formula.
3. Select **Tools | Formula Auditing | Trace Precedents**.
   Arrows appear on the worksheet which indicate the cells used as input to the NPV formula.
   The cell range *H2:H13* is surrounded by a border and a single arrow indicates that the values in all of these cells are used.

	A	B	C	D	E	F	G	H
1		Incoming	Outgoing	Profit	Rounded Profit	Trend		Savings
2	Jan	6745	-3262.16	3482.84	3500			-848.284
3	Feb	3195	-2137.22	1057.78	1100	DOWN		-105.778
4	Mar	2620	-2014.68	605.32	600	DOWN		-60.532
5	Apr	2375	-1909.06	465.94	500	DOWN		-46.594
6	May	5940	-2879.74	3060.26	3100	UP		-306.026
7	Jun	5385	-2794.24	2590.76	2600	DOWN		-259.076
8	Jul	6835	-3139.98	3695.02	3700	UP		-369.502
9	Aug	5995	-2997.94	2997.06	3000	DOWN		-299.706
10	Sep	2365	-1856.26	508.74	500	DOWN		-50.874
11	Oct	1925	-1739.02	185.98	200	DOWN		-18.598
12	Nov	4220	-2571.16	1648.84	1600	UP		-164.884
13	Dec	2650	-2052	598	600	DOWN		-59.8
14								
15	Annual Total:		20896.54					
16								
17	Outgoing Total:		-29353.5					
18	Discount Rate:	0.0046833						
19	NPV:	-2,034.93						
20	Fixed sum:	-150						
21	PV:	1,747.50						
22								
23	Fixed sum:	-200						
24	Interest rate:	0.00625						
25	FV:	2,484.24						
26	PMT:	-274.56						
27								
28	Rate:	1.26%						
29								

Note: To remove the trace arrows you have added to your worksheet, select **Tools | Formula Auditing | Remove All Arrows**.

Tracing dependent cells

You could have worked out the precedent cells for any formula by reading the formula. You could have simply read the precedent cells from the formula itself. More intimidating is the idea of trying to find out if a particular cell is used by any formula in your spreadsheet, without checking each formula individually! But again, Excel offers you a handy function to do just that.

Excel's **Trace Dependents** command indicates the cells containing formulae that refer to a selected cell.

Note: Trace Dependents can only find dependent cells on the same worksheet as the selected cell. If there are dependencies on other worksheets, or in other *open* workbooks, a black arrow to a worksheet icon is shown on the current worksheet to let you know that a dependency exists, but the specific cells are not identified. If a formula in a closed workbook refers to the selected cell, you must open that workbook for Excel to establish that a dependency exists.

In the next exercise, you will trace the dependent cells for one of the monthly profit totals on the *PROFIT* worksheet of MFPF_FINANCE.XLS (or Ex18.2-MFPF_FINANCE.xls).

Exercise 18.4: Tracing dependent cells

1. Open MFPF_FINANCE.XLS (or Ex18.2-MFPF_FINANCE.xls) and go to the *OUTGOING* worksheet.
2. Select cell *B5*.
3. Select **Tools | Formula Auditing | Trace Dependents**.
   Arrows appear on the worksheet to indicate the cells that use cell *B5* as an input.

   Note: Cell *C15* is a dependent of cell *B5*. Cell *C15* is itself a precedent of cell *C15* on the *PROFIT* worksheet. If a dependent cell is itself a precedent cell for the formula in another cell, no arrow appears to indicate this. You will need to check each dependent cell for further dependents.

Chapter summary

Excel allows you to identify the cells in a worksheet that contain formulae using the **Go To** command, or by switching between displaying formulae and the values they generate.

The **Trace Precedents** command locates all of the cells referred to by the formula in a selected cell, and connects them to the cell containing the formula using arrows.

The **Trace Dependents** command indicates the cells in a workbook containing formulae that refer to a selected cell in the same workbook.

Quick Quiz

Circle the answer to each of the following multiple-choice questions about auditing spreadsheets.

Q1	The Go To command allows you to select only those cells on a worksheet that contain formulae.
A.	True.
B.	False.

Q2	To toggle between showing formulae and their results in cells on a spreadsheet, you can press...
A.	ALT and '.
B.	CTRL and '.
C.	ESC and '.
D.	CTRL and ALT.

Q3	To find which cells contain formulae referring to the selected cell, you use...
A.	Trace Cells.
B.	Trace Precedents.
C.	Trace Dependents.
D.	Trace Arrows.

Q4	Once you have added trace arrows to a worksheet, you must close the workbook and reopen it to remove the trace arrows again.
A.	True.
B.	False.

Q5	The Trace Dependents function can tell you if cells in other worksheets/workbooks refer to the selected cell.
A.	True.
B.	False.

Answers **1:** A; **2:** B; **3:** C; **4:** B; **5:** A.

Chapter 19: Sharing and protecting your spreadsheets

In this chapter

There are a variety of reasons you might want to share your spreadsheet with other people: for information purposes only, or so that they can add specific data that you need then return it, for example.

When you give copies of your spreadsheets to other people for information purposes, you may want them to see final values in all of the cells, but not the formulae used to generate them.

If you want someone to add specific data, you might want them to fill in certain values and see a result calculated. You don't want them to change the formulae used, or edit any existing data: you just want them to be able to edit a few specific cells.

In this chapter, you will look at different ways you can protect all or part of a workbook before sharing it with someone else.

New skills

At the end of this chapter you should be able to:

- Hide and unhide columns and rows in a worksheet
- Hide and unhide worksheets in a workbook
- Protect individual cells in a worksheet
- Apply password protection to worksheets and workbooks

New words

There are no new words in this chapter.

Syllabus reference

The following syllabus items are covered in this chapter:
- AM 4.1.2.2 – Hide / unhide rows or columns.
- AM 4.1.2.3 – Hide / unhide worksheets.

- AM 4.1.3.1 – Protect / unprotect a worksheet with a password.
- AM 4.1.3.2 – Protect / unprotect designated cells in a worksheet with a password.
- AM 4.1.4.1 – Add password protection to a spreadsheet.
- AM 4.1.4.2 – Remove password protection from a spreadsheet.

Hiding columns and rows

You can hide individual columns and rows in any Excel worksheet.

After hiding a column or row, you will need to password-protect either the worksheet or the workbook containing the hidden column or row, otherwise anyone can unhide the column or row at any time.

Hiding a column

Joe Molloy, from Joe's Hardware, lost the books he kept his order records in, so he needs to recreate them. He has asked Mr Murphy for a copy of the delivery records he kept. Mr Murphy has agreed, and asks you to give Joe a copy of the *DELIVERIES* worksheet of DELIVERIES.XLS. Before handing it over, though, you should hide the column that shows the petrol cost for each delivery.

In the next exercise, you will hide column D on the *DELIVERIES* worksheet of DELIVERIES.XLS (or Ex11.4-DELIVERIES.xls), which shows the cost of petrol for each delivery.

Exercise 19.1: Hiding a column

1. Open DELIVERIES.XLS (or Ex11.4-DELIVERIES.xls), and go to the *DELIVERIES* worksheet.
2. Select column D.
3. Select **Format | Column | Hide**.
   The column disappears.
   You can see the location of the hidden column, because the columns in the worksheet now go: *A, B, C, E, F, ...*

	A	B	C	E
1	DeliveryDate	CompanyName	Delivery charge	
2	Jan-00	Mullens	10	
3	Jan-00	Liam Kinsella and Sons	10	
4	Jan-00	Joe's Hardware	5	

Unhiding a column

In the next exercise you will unhide the column you hid in *Exercise 19.1*.

Exercise 19.2: Unhiding a column

1. Open DELIVERIES.XLS (or Ex19.1-DELIVERIES.xls), and go to the *DELIVERIES* worksheet.
2. Select the columns either side of the hidden column, in this case columns *C* and *E*.
3. Select **Format | Column | Unhide**.
   Column *D* reappears.
4. Save and close your workbook when you are done.

Note: If column *A* is hidden, you cannot use the above method to unhide it since there is no column to the left of it to select. Instead type *A1* in the *Name Box* at the top of the spreadsheet and press **Enter**. Then you can select **Format | Column | Unhide** to show the hidden column.

Hiding and unhiding rows

The procedures for hiding and unhiding rows are the same, except that you select the **Row** option on the **Format** menu instead of the **Column** option, for example, **Format | Row | Hide**.

Hiding worksheets

As well as hiding individual rows and columns in a worksheet, you can select a whole worksheet and hide it from view in your workbook.

Joe Molloy has asked the Murphys to send him his invoices by e-mail in future. They have agreed to send him a copy of the Excel spreadsheet for each invoice.

The invoice template you use, INVOICE_MFPF.XLT, contains two worksheets: *Customer Invoice*, and *Personal Notes*. When you pass an invoice on to Joe, you will want to hide the *Personal Notes* worksheet first.

In the next exercise, you will hide the *Personal Notes* worksheet of INVOICE1.XLS (or Ex2.1-INVOICE1.xls).

Exercise 19.3: Hiding a worksheet

1. Open INVOICE1.XLS (or Ex2.1-INVOICE1.xls) and go to the *Personal Notes* worksheet.
2. Select **Format | Sheet | Hide**.
   The *Personal Notes* worksheet disappears.
3. Save the workbook.

You have hidden a whole worksheet in your workbook.

Unhiding worksheets

To unhide worksheets in a workbook, you open a dialog box which lists all of the hidden worksheets in the book, and select the one to unhide.

In the next exercise, you will unhide the worksheet you hid in *Exercise 19.3*.

Exercise 19.4: Unhiding a worksheet

1. Open INVOICE1.XLS (or Ex19.3-INVOICE1.xls).
2. Select **Format | Sheet | Unhide...**.
   The *Unhide* dialog box appears.

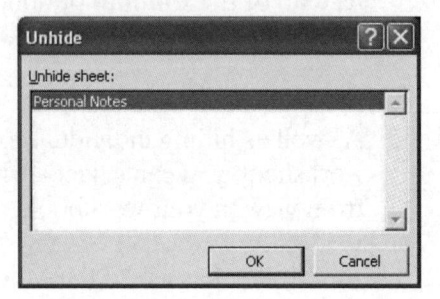

3. The *Unhide* dialog box lists all of the hidden worksheets in the current workbook.
   Select *Personal Notes*, and click **OK**.
   The *Personal Notes* worksheet reappears.
4. Finally, repeat the steps in *Exercise 19.3* to hide the worksheet again.

Note: Unless you password-protect your workbook, Joe will be able to unhide the worksheet again just like you did in this exercise. You will learn about password-protecting workbooks in *Protecting workbooks* on page 218.

Protecting cells

When you share a spreadsheet with other people, you can prevent them from making any changes to it, or you can restrict them to changing certain cells only.

If you are issuing an invoice, you will not want the customer to be able to change any of the details in the invoice. If you are using a spreadsheet as an order form, on the other hand, you will want the customer to be able to enter a quantity for each product, but not change the product list or prices.

You can assign two types of protection to a cell:

- *Locked*: If a cell is locked, you cannot edit the cell's contents.
- *Hidden*: If a cell is hidden, you can see the value in the cell, but if a formula was used to calculate the value, you cannot see the formula.

By default, Excel assumes that you want all cells to be locked, but not hidden, when you protect a worksheet or workbook.

Note: The protection setting for a cell is not enforced until you protect the worksheet or workbook containing the cell.

Specifying protection settings for a cell

Joe Molloy has asked you to leave an editable area in the electronic copies of the invoices you send him, where he can enter the date he paid the invoice. Remember, by default all cells will be locked when you password-protect your workbook.

In the next exercise you will set the protection for a cell on the *Customer Invoice* worksheet of INVOICE1.XLS (or Ex19.4-INVOICE1.xls) so that Joe can enter into it the date the invoice was paid.

Exercise 19.5: Setting protection for a cell

1. Open INVOICE1.XLS (or Ex19.4-INVOICE1.xls) and go to the *Customer Invoice* worksheet.
2. In cell *E30*, enter the label *Date paid:*.
3. Select cell *F30*.
4. Select **Format | Cells...**.
   The *Format Cells* dialog box opens.
5. Click the **Protection** tab.

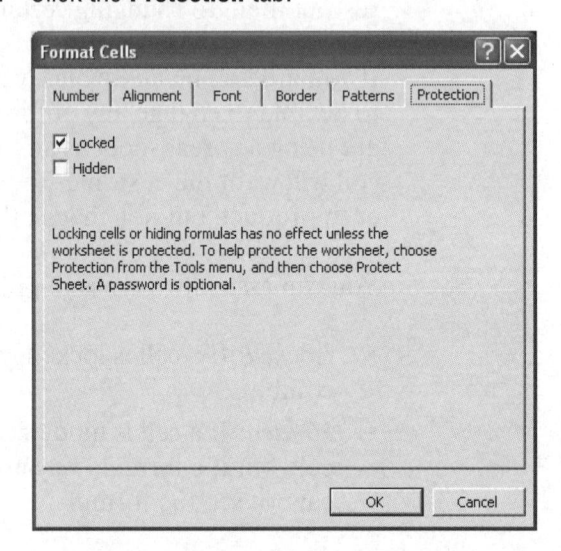

6. Ensure that the checkboxes beside *Locked* and *Hidden* are *not* selected, then click **OK**.
   Cell *F30* is now unprotected so that even after password protection has been added to the worksheet, or workbook, the value in this cell can be edited.

Protecting worksheets

To protect the contents of a worksheet, and to enforce the protection settings applied to cells within it, you will need to protect the sheet itself. You can choose to protect a worksheet with or without a password, but if you do not use a password, then anyone can unprotect the worksheet again.

When you protect a worksheet, the locked and hidden settings for each individual cell are used – remember that by default all cells are *Locked* and none are *Hidden*: for cells whose protection settings you have manually edited, the custom protection settings are used instead. In addition, you are provided with a list of possible actions users of the worksheet might try to carry out, and you can allow or disallow each action individually. Examples of such actions are formatting cells or deleting columns.

In the next exercise you will protect the contents of the *Customer Invoice* worksheet of INVOICE1.XLS (or Ex19.5-INVOICE1.xls).

Exercise 19.6: Protecting a worksheet

1. Open INVOICE1.XLS (or Ex19.5-INVOICE1.xls) and go to the *Customer Invoice* worksheet.

2. Select **Tools | Protection | Protect Sheet...**.
   The *Protect Sheet* dialog box opens.

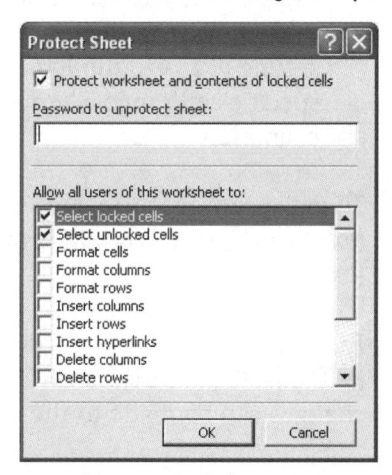

3. By default, users of the workbook are allowed to *Select locked cells* and *Select unlocked cells*, but cannot perform other actions.
   You may choose to add or remove other permissions if you like, but in order for Joe Molloy to add his details to the cell you unprotected for him, you'll have to leave at least the *Select unlocked cells* option turned on.

4. Enter a password in the *Password* field, and click **OK**.
   The *Confirm Password* dialog box opens.

5. Re-enter your password and click **OK**.

You can unprotect the worksheet again at any time by selecting **Tools | Protection | Unprotect sheet** and entering the password you used to protect it. If you didn't specify a password, the worksheet is unprotected immediately.

Protecting workbooks

You can hide or protect individual worksheets in a workbook, but you can still unhide, add and delete worksheets (even protected ones) as long as the workbook itself is unprotected.

You can choose to protect two different aspects of a workbook:

- *Structure*: If you protect the structure of a workbook, you cannot add, remove, hide or unhide worksheets. Also, you cannot unhide rows or columns, or change the protection on cells or worksheets.
- *Windows*: If you protect the windows, then the size and location on the screen of the workbook will be the same every time it is opened. You might want to use this setting to resize the Excel window to exactly frame a specific cell range when a workbook is opened, for example.

To make sure that Joe does not unhide and read the *Personal Notes* worksheet, you will protect the workbook containing his invoice.

In the next exercise, you will assign password protection to INVOICE1.XLS (or Ex19.6-INVOICE1.xls), so that no further changes can be made to the workbook.

Exercise 19.7: Protecting a workbook

1. Open INVOICE1.XLS (or Ex19.6-INVOICE1.xls).
2. Select **Tools | Protection | Protect Workbook...**.
   The *Protect Workbook* dialog box opens.

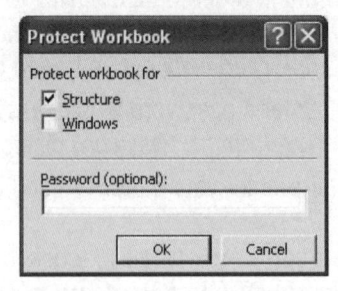

3. Check the checkbox beside *Structure* and uncheck the one beside *Windows*.

4. Enter a password in the *Password* field and click **OK**. The *Confirm Password* dialog box opens.
5. Re-enter your password and click **OK**.
6. Save and close your workbook when you are done.

You can remove the protection again by selecting **Tools | Protection | Unprotect Workbook** and entering the password you used to protect the workbook. As with unprotecting worksheets, if you didn't specify a password, the workbook is unprotected immediately when you select this command.

Chapter summary

You can hide individual columns and rows in any Excel worksheet. You can also select a whole worksheet and hide it from view in your workbook.

You can protect any cell against editing, or hide formulae in cells, so that only the final calculated value can be seen.

When you protect a worksheet, the cell protection settings you assigned are applied and you can also choose from a list of formatting and editing options which actions a user of the workbook should be allowed to perform and which ones they shouldn't.

You can choose to protect a workbook's structure so that you cannot add, remove, hide or unhide worksheets, unhide rows or columns, or change the protection on cells or worksheets. You can also protect a workbook so that its size and location on the screen of the workbook will be the same every time it is opened.

Quick Quiz

Circle the answer to each of the following multiple-choice questions about sharing and protecting spreadsheets.

Q1	You cannot select a cell in a hidden row/column.
A.	True.
B.	False.

Q2	You cannot unhide a worksheet unless you know where it was originally positioned relative to the remaining unhidden worksheets.
A.	True.
B.	False.

Q3	As soon as you set the protection for a cell to hidden, the cell cannot be viewed by users of the worksheet.
A.	True.
B.	False.

Q4	If you don't specify a password when protecting a worksheet/workbook, the user who tries to unprotect it still needs to know that they should specify a blank password in order to unprotect it.
A.	True.
B.	False.

Q5	You can specify that protected workbooks should always open to the same size and location on a user's screen.
A.	True.
B.	False.

Answers **1:** B; **2:** B; **3:** B; **4:** B; **5:** A.

In conclusion

Now that you have completed all the tasks in this book, you have completed the required syllabus for ECDL Advanced Spreadsheets, and are able to:

- Save time on repetitive tasks by using templates and macros
- Keep track of the data in your spreadsheets by using named cells and cell ranges, comments, and auditing
- Reuse data by importing it from text files and databases, using different Paste Special options, and creating links between spreadsheets or from Word documents
- Make your data easier to read by performing multi-column sorts, applying cell and worksheet formatting, customising charts, and summarising large amounts of information in PivotTables
- Use key reference, maths, statistics, database, finance, text, date, time, and logical functions
- Consider how changing the value of a variable will affect your calculations by using data tables and scenarios
- Protect your work against being edited by protecting cells, workbooks and worksheets

Also, thanks to your hard work, the Murphys now have a comprehensive set of spreadsheets that show their sales data for the year, and track their financial incomings and outgoings. Hopefully the bank manager will now approve their loan, and based on the comparative information you have provided them with, they will invest wisely for the future.

Congratulations, you have done a great job!

Appendix: Advanced spreadsheets test

In this section

The follow test allows you to check your knowledge of the advanced spreadsheet features in Excel. The test uses the spreadsheet course.xls on the CD accompanying this book.

The test

1. Open the spreadsheet course.xls, and on the *Students* worksheet apply the autoformat *List 2*.
2. On the *Students* worksheet, perform a multiple column sort that sorts the data by *Course* in ascending order, then by *Name* in ascending order.
3. On the *Students* worksheet, apply conditional formatting to column *C* so that entries with the value *F* are displayed in bold pink, and entries with the value *M* are displayed in bold blue.
4. The spreadsheet course.xls contains a hidden worksheet called *Fees*. Unhide this worksheet.
5. On the *Students* worksheet, enter a vlookup formula in cell *G2* that finds the appropriate BA fee for the current student's enrolment type in the table on the *Fees* worksheet.
   Hint: Look for an exact match in the table on the *Fees* worksheet.
   Copy the formula to cells *G3:G14*.
   Enter a similar formula for MSc students in the cell range *G15:G23*, and for PhD students in the cell range *G24:G26*.
6. On the *Students* worksheet, add a comment to cell *H1* that says:
   Fees should be paid in full before enrollment. A late fee applies to course fees paid after the start of the academic year.
7. On the *Fees* worksheet, record a macro called *Titles* that freezes column A and row 1 and formats their contents in bold italics.
8. On the *Fees* worksheet, name cell *B7 Late*.
9. On the *Students* worksheet, enter a function in cell *H2* that checks if the student paid their fees late (indicated by a *Y* in column *E*) and if so increases the total amount due by the percentage specified in named cell *Late* on the *Fees* worksheet.

If the student paid on time, the value in this cell should be the same as that in cell *G2*. Copy the formula to cells *H3:H26*.

10. On the *Students* worksheet, edit the *Enrolment* value for student *Wayne Stewart* to say *International*, then update the PivotTable on the *Student Statistics* worksheet to reflect the change.

11. On the *Students* worksheet, calculate subtotals by course for the total fees in column *H*.

12. On the *Students* worksheet, select the non-adjacent cell range *F15,H15,F25,H25,F29,H29* and create a pie chart from the data, adding it on a new worksheet called *Fees Totals*.
    On the *Fees Totals* worksheet, rotate the chart clockwise so that the *PhD* slice begins at the 12 o'clock position.

13. On the *Fees Totals* worksheet, explode the slices in the pie chart.

14. On the *Fees* worksheet, starting at cell *A8* add a link to the non-adjacent cell range *F15,H15,F25,H25,F29,H29* on the *Students* worksheet.

15. On the *Fees* worksheet, in cell *C8* enter a function that rounds the value in cell *B8* to the nearest thousand. Copy the function to cells *C9* and *C10*.

16. On the *Fees* worksheet, create two named scenarios as follows:

Scenario name	Changing cells	Cell	Value
2002	D2:D4,B6	D2	0
		D3	4000
		D4	9000
		B6	10%

Scenario name	Changing cells	Cell	Value
2003	D2:D4,B6	D2	0
		D3	4500
		D4	10500
		B6	15%

17. On the *Fees* worksheet, create a scenario summary report using the scenarios created in step16, with results cells *B8:B10*.
18. On the *Students* worksheet, display all formulas used.
19. On the *Students* worksheet, trace the precedents for the formula in cell *H2*.
20. On the *Fees* worksheet, password protect the cells in the non-adjacent cell range *B2:D4,B6* with the password ECDL in uppercase letters.
Save and close your workbook when you are finished.

Index

absolute cell references 122
absolute macros 109–10, 115
adaptive menus 3–4
AND function 28–32, 184–9
arrow sign in a worksheet 208
auditings 203–4, 221
AutoFill 41
AutoFormat 98–9, 105

blank cells, treatment of 63–6
boilerplate text 6, 11

capitalization of letters 176–9
charts 136–49
   adding data series to 136
   deleting data series from 136–9, 149
   formatting of axes 140–1
   inserting pictures in 142–4
   legends on 148–9
   linkage with source data 85, 91–3
   modifying types of 139–40, 149
   widening of gaps between columns 141–2, 149
colour format codes 101
column titles, freezing of 96–8, 105
comments 51–4, 61, 221
concatenation 177–9
conditional formatting 101–5, 183
copying files from CD 3
COUNT function 152–3, 159
COUNTA function 153, 159
COUNTIF function 154, 159
counting of cells in specified ranges 151

criteria
   addition of 31–3
   for import of data records 8
   for specifying database fields 151, 155
   for specifying database rows to be counted 158–9
   for summation 129–30
criteria fields 30
cross-workbook links 88–9
custom lists 40–4
custom names for cells and cell ranges 47–51, 54, 86
   and formulae 49–51, 54
custom number formats 99–102, 105
custom protection settings 216
custom sort orders 40–4
custom toolbar button 114–15

data tables 191–6, 200–1, 221
   1-input type 192–5, 200
   2-input type 192, 195–6, 200–1
databases
   data imported from 21–4
   in Excel 151, 154, 159
   functions used with 154–9
date formats 112
date functions 175, 178–9
DAY function 179
DCOUNT function 158–9
delimited text files 15–21, 33
dependent cells 207–8
discount rate 164, 166
#DIV/0! message 63, 189
DMAX function 157–9
DMIN function 156–9
DSUM function 155–6, 159

error messages 63, 188–9
External Data toolbar 16

FALSE results 183–9
fields in PivotTables 70–3, 81
filtering 24–33
   using Microsoft Query 29–32
   using PivotTable fields 72–3
financial functions 163–72
format codes 100–5
format pasting 61
formulae
   cell names in 49–51
   cell references in 88
   hiding of 219
   pasting of 60
freezing of row and column titles 96–8, 104
functions
   financial 163–72
   for manipulating text and date information 175
   statistical 152–4
   see also database functions; date functions; reference functions; text functions
future value of an investment 167–8, 172
FV function 167–8, 172, 193, 196–7

Go To command 127, 204–5, 208
graphics in charts 142–4, 149
grouping of objects 76–81

ECDL Advanced Spreadsheets for Microsoft® Office XP and 2003

help facilities 4
hiding
　of cells 215–16
　of columns and rows 212–13, 219
　of comments 53
　of formulae 219
　of worksheets 214–15, 219
HLOOKUP function 123–4, 132

IF function 184–5, 189
import of data 15–25, 221
　from databases 21–4, 33
　from text files 16–21
interest rate on investment 170–2
ISERROR function 188–9

legends on charts 148–9
links
　between cells 65–6, 85–6
　between cells in different workbooks or worksheets 87–8, 92–3
　between charts and source data 85, 91–3
　between spreadsheets and *Word* documents 85, 89–93, 221
locked cells 215–16
logical functions 184, 189
lookup functions 120–4
Lotus 1-2-3 153, 159
lower case letters, capitals converted to 177, 179
LOWER function 177, 179

macros 108–15, 221
mathematical functions 118–19
maximum values, location of 157–8
minimum values, location of 156–7

MONTH function 179
multiplication of numbers 118–19

nested functions 131–3, 188
net present value 164–5, 171–2
NPV function 164–5, 171–2
number formats 99–102, 105

OR function 28–32, 187–9
overwriting of data 60

parameters in functions 121
passwords 212, 215–19
Paste Link option (in Paste Special) 65–6
Paste Special command 57–66, 221
　and mathematics 118–19
　special options for 63–5
　used for linking *Excel* with *Word* 89–93
pie charts 144–9
PivotTables 69–81, 221
PMT function 168–72
precedent cells 206–8
present value of an investment 166–7, 172
PROPER function 176, 179
protection
　of cells, workbooks and worksheets 211, 215–21
　of windows 218
PURECOUNT function (in Lotus 1-2-3) 153, 159
PV function 166–7, 172

qualifiers 17
queries 21–33
　creation of 22–4
　editing of 26–9
　saving of 25–9
　use of filters and sorts in 24–5

Query Wizard 29, 33
quotation marks, use of 17, 176, 178

RATE function 170–2
reference functions 119–24
refreshing of data 16, 80–1
relative cell references 122
relative macros 110, 115
Reviewing Toolbar 51, 53
round brackets, use of 131
rounding of numbers 130–2
row titles, freezing of 96–8, 104–5

scenarios 191, 196–201, 221
scrolling through a spreadsheet 96–7
sharing of spreadsheets 211
showing of comments 53
Skip Blanks option (in Paste Special) 63–6
sorting of data records 24–8, 33, 38–44, 221
　custom orders for 40–4
　in multiple columns 38–9, 44
space-delimited text files 18–21
square brackets, use of 88
statistical functions 152–4
strings of text 176–9
subtotalling 124–7, 132
SUM function 127–8, 132
SUMIF function 128–30, 132
summarization of data 69–70, 221
SUMPOSITIVE function 130

templates 6–11, 221
text files
　delimited 15–21, 33
　structured 16–17

text functions 175–8
Text Import Wizard 16–17, 21, 33
text qualifiers 17
three-dimensional (3D) summation 127–8
TODAY function 178–9
totals, calculation of 124–30
Trace Dependents command 207–8
Trace Precedents command 206–8
transposition (in Paste Special) 64–6

triangle sign in a cell 51, 54
TRUE results 183–9

unhiding
  of columns and rows 212–13
  of worksheets 213–14, 218
unprotection of workbooks and worksheets 217, 219
UPPER function 176–9
user actions allowed or disallowed 216, 219

visible cells, selection of 127
Visual Basic 109

VLOOKUP function 120–2, 132

'what if?' calculations 191
Word documents linked to spreadsheets 85, 89–93, 221

YEAR function 179

zero, division by 63
zero (0) code 101

Licensing Agreement

This book comes with a CD. By opening this package, you are agreeing to be bound by the following:

The files contained on this CD are copyrighted. THIS CD IS PROVIDED FREE OF CHARGE, AS IS, AND WITHOUT WARRANTY OF ANY KIND, EITHER EXPRESSED OR IMPLIED, INCLUDING, BUT NOT LIMITED TO, THE IMPLIED WARRANTIES OF MERCHANTABILITY AND FITNESS FOR A PARTICULAR PURPOSE. Neither the book publisher nor its dealers and its distributors assumes any liability for any alleged or actual damages arising for the use of this software.